CHOOSE CHANGE

Take control, achieve your goals, and create the life you want

CHOOSE CHANGE

Take control, achieve your goals, and create the life you want

By
Angela M. Garvin

Copyright © 2018 Angela M. Garvin

All rights reserved. No part of this publication may be reproduced, distributed, or transmitted in any for or by any means, including photocopying, recording, or other electronic or mechanical methods, without prior written permission of the publisher, except in the case of brief quotations embodied in reviews and certain other noncommercial one word uses permitted by copyright law.

Published by Angela M. Garvin

Cover design by Happy Self Publishing,
www.happyselfpublishing.com

Editor: Carrie Ludwig

Proofreader: Tammi Metzler,
www.WriteAssociate.com

Formatter: Happy Self Publishing,
www.happyselfpublishing.com

DEDICATION

for Norma

Grandma, you have inspired me more than I can ever express.

Your encouragement, support and love has carried me through the many changes of my life.

Thank you for being my cheerleader and loving me the way you have.

TABLE OF CONTENTS

Hello, Reader ix

Introduction Start Dreaming...1

Chapter 1: Begin Today..13

Chapter 2: Utilize Time.. 27

Chapter 3: Life Happens... 43

Chapter 4: Dynamic Plans 57

Chapter 5: Choose Your Attitude.......................................71

Chapter 6: Progress Over Perfection 85

Chapter 7: Find Your People..101

Chapter 8: Follow Through 115

Chapter 9: Celebrate Effort..129

Chapter 10: Choose Joy 141

Chapter 11: Routine Power 153

Chapter 12: Ask For Help 167

Chapter 13: Get Radical 179

Chapter 14: Pay It Forward... 191

Conclusion: Take Ownership 203

Message from the Author 211

Chapter Challenges 215

Quote Inspiration 223

Acknowledgements 225

About the Author 227

Resources 229

HELLO, READER

I am thrilled to meet you. We don't know each other, but I want to take a moment to tell you something.

I want you to be successful. You can be.

I don't know where you are in life or what you are struggling with. I don't know if you are happy or sad. I don't know what your dreams are or what your situation is. What I do know is that I want you to have the best life you can have and to realize you are capable of achieving that. No matter what your challenges are, I believe you are capable of more than you have ever dreamed of. Maybe you doubt that right now. Perhaps you are so filled with self-doubt that you can't even breathe and have no idea what you should do next. You may feel stuck. You may feel trapped. Or maybe you just need a push in the right direction. I can understand all of those feelings, believe me. As I have been going through the process of writing this book, I have experienced more self-doubt than I ever have before. I have had this dream of writing a book in my mind for so many years, but I always wondered what I would say and if anyone would even care to read it. And as I am writing this, I still don't have an answer to that question.

However, I do know this.

I am capable of more than I have ever dreamed. I am capable of accomplishing the things that keep me up at night and keep me dreaming. Not because I am some big shot, because I'm not. And not because I am wealthy and powerful; neither of those descriptions fit me either. I am capable of it because I have the ability to make the choices that get me where I want to go. I have the ability to choose the things that matter, to focus on things that make a difference, get me further and make an impact.

I have that choice. And so do you.

I am not going to lie; changing your life is hard. Taking on new projects and switching the direction of your life is fraught with challenges and frustrations. However, you and I are capable of making our dreams happen because we have the power to make choices that get us closer to the end goal. I am so grateful to you for picking up this book and taking the time to read it. Your life matters to me. I hope you can see that throughout this book, because it is true. I want to pump confidence and truth into you, so you become more self-assured, take a step forward to your goals and begin changing your life in positive ways. Before you start, I want you to read the following out loud to yourself.

I am capable of change.
I am capable of bettering my life and the lives of those around me.
I am capable of personal growth.
I am capable of making things happen.

You are important to me, truly. I am so excited to go on this journey with you and see where it takes you.

Always,
Angela

Change is hard at first, messy in the middle and gorgeous at the end.

~ Robin Sharma

INTRODUCTION

START DREAMING

If your life could look drastically different, how would you want it to look? What would your career be? What would your social life be like? Would you be single? Would you have a few adorable children? Would you be healthier? Wealthier? More content? Financially stable? Less anxious or depressed? Would you live nearer to your family? Or maybe move to another state, or even a different country? Would you travel more or maybe find a way to spend extra time closer to home? The list of questions could go on and on, and believe me, I am tempted to continue.

I want you to start thinking about this seriously. But not just that; I also want you to think about this on a deeper level. I know we all think about what our lives could look like if we do one thing or another. However, we often dismiss these thoughts, these plans, and these desires because it is easier to stay where we are and who we are, even if we hate it. Depressing thought, don't you think? You know it is true, though. Often, we find ourselves staying where we are because frankly, change takes a great deal of work. It takes thought. It takes time and effort. And sometimes we just honestly don't feel like it is worth the effort to try.

I have been in that position many, many times. It is a natural feeling we all have, myself included, but it is one we need to fight against. We need to stop giving in to this idea of staying in the same place because it is easy. Why?

Because it gets us absolutely nowhere near where we want or hope to be. And that, my friends, is a horrible way to live your life. I do not want that for your life. You could have so much better, and we both know it.

The subject of change has been a huge focus in my adult life. It started out of desperation but grew into a way of living for me. The focus on change, becoming better, and continuing to learn and challenge myself, is something that makes my heart skip a beat. I love things that are easy, simple, uncomplicated and free of stress and drama as much as the next person. At the same time, though, I embrace this idea that tomorrow I could be different. I could be a better version of myself. Though it may not be visible to those around me in that moment, I know it. I feel it. And it propels me to continue on and fight for even more change.

When I was twenty-two years old, I was coming out of a very dark time in my life. I had made some mistakes that set me back and made life more challenging than it should have been. It was a hard time for sure. I wanted to give up and just let whatever happened, happen. The desire to just give in was still strong at that point, but I also knew I had options. I had choices. I had a chance. Even though I struggled (and still do) with depression and anxiety, I knew life could be better, and I wanted to find out how that might look. I was curious what life could look like outside of my bubble of frustration, self-loathing and depression.

So I set out to make that happen.

At that point in time, my main focus was on being observant of what was going on in my life. What were my friends like? What was work like? How did I interact with my friends and family? I wanted to learn as much as I could about my current situation so I could make smarter decisions moving forward. I wanted to be aware of what was going on with my life, if I was truly happy with how I was living, what other people were doing, and any other information I could get my hands on.

Around this time in my life, I started to realize that some of the friendships I had were anything but healthy. I felt very alone, as if I was living in the background of life. Being the introvert that I am, living that way isn't always a bad thing, but I do love people. I love interaction. I love connecting with others and finding ways to make them laugh and enjoy their day. Being able to make someone smile or laugh when they aren't expecting it or being a listening ear for a stranger are both things I cherish about being around people. However, at that time in my life, I lacked those kinds of interactions, and my friendships were not very healthy; they lacked what I needed. I knew that the relationships I had needed to change in order for me to survive and thrive, but it did not happen overnight.

It was a slow process, and it has happened a few times over the course of my life. As I began to change, my friendships began to as well. Friends phased out of my life, whether by my doing, by their own, or just by the natural progression of life. I was changing the course of my life, and some people just didn't come along for the ride.

I also began to realize that my life was starting to go down a new path that was destructive for me. I had just come out of a bad situation and was starting to put my life back together when I found myself starting to drink alcohol. Going from one time a week to a few times a week, I quickly realized that my life was headed in a direction I did not want to go. I was using alcohol to be comfortable around people, and I knew that I needed to regain control. I needed to change what I was doing or risk losing the progress I had made and possibly find myself down yet another dark path I would have to claw my way out of.

Change begins when we step back and look at our situation with clear eyes, which means being honest with ourselves about what is going on. Change begins when we can see who and where we truly are and realize that much of the blame lies on ourselves. Not terribly fun, I know, but it is the beginning of the process. Once I was able to step back and look at my life honestly in the moment, I was able to make a decision that I believe ultimately saved me from a life of struggling with alcoholism. Was it hard? Yes. It still is, if I am going to be completely honest here. That insight into myself and my addictive tendencies saved me a lot of pain in the future.

Change is not a word most of us like, myself included. As I said, it takes effort and energy to change, and so often we choose not to do the work we need to do to make our lives what we want them to be. Or we focus on certain parts of our lives with everything we have, but then let other areas of our lives that are just as important wither and become less than what they could be.

However, change is necessary when it comes to our growth as individuals. And if we are honest with ourselves, change is something we all want! We have all wanted to change one of our relationships, our career path, or where we work. We have all wanted to change our body, to become healthier or to get more toned. We have all wanted our financial situation to change, whether it is to pay off our debt, save a million dollars for retirement, have the cash flow to travel around the world or have the ability to be outrageously generous.

We all desire change; we just don't always want to do the work it takes to make that change happen. So, we choose not to do it. We choose not to step forward and see what our lives could look like if we try.

Change can be defined as becoming different. The act of becoming different.[1] The *act*. And no, we are not talking about acting in a play, putting on some performance or being fake as all get-out.

The act of becoming different, and changing your life, is taking action.

In other words, change is a matter of effort, not fate or happenstance. Yes, there are those times in our lives when good things happen out of the blue. Winning the lottery is the "go-to" example here for sure. It does happen, but it is so rare that it is something that no one can count on.

For the past few months, I have realized that many of my thoughts have revolved around how much today matters, and how the action I am taking, or failing to follow through on, counts for or against me in the big picture. The results I want in life are not going to happen overnight.

We have discussed the word "change" already. Let's look at "progression" before we move forward. The dictionary defines progression as "the process of developing or moving gradually towards a more advanced state."[2]

We all want to go somewhere, don't we? We all want to advance. Of course we do, but did you notice the catch in there? It is a particular word that we need to remember when it comes to this process.

Gradual.

Therein lies the rub. Yes, successes can happen at a faster pace; it is not entirely impossible. In this day and age, that is more of a possibility than it ever has been before. Many things in our lives have become more "instant," but we have to remember and maybe even re-realize that much of life does not work that way. Overnight success is a myth, as success most often happens in stages. You don't lose fifty pounds overnight unless you're chopping off body parts. You don't become a millionaire in a day unless you are one of the rare winners of the lottery or happen to come into another lump sum of cash. There is a lot of effort that goes into change.

And that is where the power of progression and changing our life in stages comes in. It is so powerful that it can change your existence if you just allow it to do so.

Life happens in stages. No matter how much we want to get to our ultimate goal faster, it doesn't work that way. We get there in steps, a progression of events, strategies, and plans we don't just plan out but execute and execute often.

The truth is that you hold the responsibility to changing your life, your situation, your existence. I know it is much easier to lay the blame and burden on others; it is definitely more convenient. However, it is not someone else's responsibility to change your current situation.

It is yours.

It is your job to embrace not only the change but the challenge that comes with it. It is your job, and my job as well, to latch on and face the work that needs to be done in order to get to the life that we want. It is our job to take those steps, ask the questions, make plans and push forward. And to be relentless about it.

I want you to take a minute right now to think about what your life could look like or what you want it to look like. What are you doing? Who is around? How are you helping others? How are you taking care of yourself? Where are you living? How much money do you have in the bank?

I want to make sure that one thing is very clear: I do not believe that possessions are the epitome of success. Money doesn't solve all your problems. Having the newest car or the biggest house is never going to make you truly happy. However, I don't accept that desiring those things is always wrong. It comes down to how you get to that point of success, how you treat others along your journey, and how you use the blessings you were given. We are meant to be diligent in our work, chase after goals and grow as people. And as you grow and change, the rest of your life will evolve as well.

Think about the picture you have put together in your mind. Is it doable? Possible? My guess is, most definitely yes. Much of what we want in life is possible and not beyond all reason, more so than we realize. We will discuss that throughout this book. For now, I want you to focus on the dreaming side of things. I want you to take some time and imagine this picture of life that you have in your mind. It is dreaming time. It is time for you to think big and broad. Include it all, and don't leave anything out.

What is on your list?

I want to challenge you to embrace this process. I want you to dig in and analyze your life in ways you never have before. I want you to push forward and accomplish what you have never dreamed you could. I want that for you so badly. If you knew me well, you would know that when I say I want the best for you, I mean it.

I don't want you to settle or to be a victim in life. I don't want you to let life happen to you or choose mediocrity just because it is easier than trying.

I want you to dream. I want you to put in the effort. I want you to realize your dreams and experience the adventures that have been put on your heart. I believe you can do this. I really do. Change is not the easiest thing in the world. Change is sometimes super exciting, and at times it takes every ounce of your being to push through the frustration. Change—especially serious, big, life-altering change—is not for the faint of heart. However, I do not accept for a second that it is beyond what you are capable of.

You are important to me. I don't know who you are, or what your name is, but you are important to me. I want to help you achieve the goals you have, help you transform your life. In big or small ways, I want to help you get there. It is what is on my heart. I want the best for you, and I hope and pray that is what you want for yourself, too. You must; you're still reading, right?

You can change your life. You can be in a new location, a new job, a better relationship, an improved marriage. You can become debt-free, or whatever else you want to achieve. These are possible.

Are you ready to dive in? I hope so.

This is going to be an awesome journey. If you commit to the challenge, you are going to transform your life.

Let's get this party started, shall we?

Chapter review:

Change is a matter of effort—not fate or happenstance.

It is your job to embrace the challenge of change.

Change begins when we step back and look at our situation with clear eyes, which means being totally honest with ourselves about what is going on.

It is not someone else's responsibility to change your current situation. It is yours.

You are capable of changing your life!

Take action challenge!

At the end of each chapter, I am going to ask you to take on a challenge! I don't want you just to read the words I have written; I want you to take action and start the process of changing your life. Where do we start? The best place to start: DREAMING! Take out a piece of paper and pen and start writing down the things you want to accomplish in your life.

What are your dreams? Your ambitions? Your goals? What do you want to change about your life? How would you like to improve your situation or help to improve the lives of others? Write it all down, and don't leave anything out!

Take action now!

Let today be the start of something new. The earlier you start working on something, the earlier you will see results.

CHAPTER 1

BEGIN TODAY

I am so excited that you have decided to move forward and take a step toward changing your life! It is a fantastic journey. Don't get me wrong; it is not easy to revamp your life into something you never thought possible. And not every single part of it will fill you with excitement, but rest assured, it is a very remarkable thing that is happening in your life, and I am so delighted to go along for the ride. There may be some of you who are reading this and still feel unsure, questioning your ability or your strength to make the changes you need to make. Maybe you are wondering if you are capable of the work that you need to do in order to achieve the success and the life you are looking for. I know that doubt. I know that doubt all too well, and let me fill you in on a little secret.

Everyone has that doubt.

I know, some people look like they have it all together. They have the family, the house, the career, the money, the clothes, the vacations, the social life or whatever else that makes them look like they have it all figured out. They come across like they have no doubts, no fears, and no worries. However, they are just as insecure as the rest of us in one way or another. They could have everything you have ever dreamed of having but they are still missing something, wishing for something, working for something. They also have changes they want to make in their life and things they want to improve or eliminate.

We are all in the same boat in so many ways. On the outside, it may not look like it, but the fact of the matter is that we are all fighting our own self-doubt, our pasts, and our fears.

And that is where we need to start before we begin this journey together.

The past can eat us alive sometimes, can't it? I know mine haunts me from time to time, and I am guessing yours does the same to you. It is frustrating, to say the very least. It stops you in your tracks and doesn't allow you to move forward, move on, and be free. It clings on with its claws and follows you around everywhere you go.

Like most people, I have made some decisions I either regret or am completely embarrassed by. That is just something none of us can avoid, unfortunately. One of my biggest regrets was that I stayed close to home for so long. I had a dream of moving away, out west to Portland, Oregon, to be more specific. That was my big dream. Well, a big part of it anyway. I wanted it so badly, but instead, I made decisions that kept me close to home.

Don't get me wrong; I love where I am from, minus the forty-below-zero temperatures during the winter. Those I could be completely fine living without, and I think most people would agree with that. I do love home. It holds a lot of great memories for me, and a lot of great people that I love with all of my heart. Most of my family is close by, which has allowed me to build great relationships with them that I cherish so much. That is something that would be much harder to do living farther away. I can stop over at my parents' house and visit, I get to see my nieces on a regular basis, and I have been able to stay close to my extended family. It is a blessing to be so close.

However, it was never my plan to stay. I remained in the Midwest out of fear, for the most part, and as the years passed, the regret of staying close to home, the regret of past decisions, weighed on me. Instead of doing something about it, I spent a long time continuing to make decisions that would ultimately keep me close to home, where I didn't want to be, where my heart wasn't, and that ate me up inside. I started to beat myself up mentally for all of the decisions I had made that had kept me from leaving home. I let the regret of past decisions keep me from making choices that would get me to my goal, my dream.

Instead of stepping back and realizing that I was allowing the past to destroy my future, I wallowed in the regret of what could have been. Needless to say, it didn't work well for me. I spent years wishing for a different life, but instead of taking steps forward, I stayed in the same place.

It wasn't until I was thirty-two years old that I was able to get out of my own way and finally venture out. I had just been laid off from my job of three years, and I knew I had a choice. I could stick around the area and continue on the same track as before, or I could consider moving to the place I had always wanted to be.

I chose Portland.

I gave notice at my apartment, gave up half of my stuff, packed up my little car and drove west. I had an apartment waiting for me in a neighborhood I had never been to. I was driving on roads I had never been on and doing it alone. And I had never felt more excited—or more alive—in my entire life. No longer a prisoner of my past, I realized that I still had so much living to do and that the things I longed for in life were not unrealistic, nor were they impossible.

I was doing it; it wasn't a dream anymore.

Unfortunately, my time in Portland came to an end due to an injury after only six months of living there. Despite only living there for a short time, it was still the most amazing experience, and it opened my eyes to what is possible for me. I didn't have to continue to do things the way others thought I should. I didn't have to remain somewhere just because it was what I had always done or what was easiest, though that trap is easy to fall into. I gained confidence during my time away from the Midwest that I could never have gained while close to home.

The past is just that: the past.

The past does not need to hold us prisoner but will if we allow it to. And that is the truth we need to remember: that the past is something we choose to hold onto, it is not holding onto us.

Yes, sometimes it comes back to haunt us from time to time, which can be painful, but it doesn't have to hold us back from changing our lives. It took me years to realize that, and I don't want that to be the case for you. The past does not have to be a part of everything we do or every decision we make. We have the power and ability to learn from our past decisions and move forward, making better choices to get us closer to a better existence.

Learning from what has happened can be hard, but it is vital when it comes to changing our lives for the better. It does not have to weigh us down; in fact, it is a tool for us to move forward in more efficient and intelligent ways than we have in the past.

If we would instead use our past decisions, good or bad, to help us create the future we actually want, our past becomes an ally, an asset, instead of a burden that holds us down and holds us back from living full lives. When we are no longer burdened by what has happened or wasting time regretting what has or has not occurred, we can begin to use the insights we have gained from our mistakes to move forward. And in turn, we are less likely to take the same failed roads again or duplicate our wrong decisions.

Once I was able to let go of my failures to venture out of the Midwest, I was able to let go of the chains that held me back from dreaming and living big. Though I ended up coming back home after only a short time away, I returned knowing that I was capable of taking the necessary steps to continue growing no matter where I was living. I had new insight into my life that I could use regardless of my situation, where I lived, where I was working or who I was around.

The past is the past. Or, said another way, it is what it is. That second one is my least favorite saying, but it is 100 percent true. It—whatever the "it" might be—is done. The past is something that cannot be changed or altered, as much as we might like it to be. Our regrets of the past are there, in stone, and even if we want to, we cannot chisel those choices out of existence. They remain, forever and ever.

When we spend too much time focusing on the past, it can hinder our potential to move forward, and it can cause us to lose our ability to look toward the future. The past cannot be changed, so why dwell on it? Why waste precious minutes of your life wishing certain things never happened or never came to be? Focusing on the lessons you can learn from the past is the best way of letting things go and moving forward.

It is time for you, for all of us, to focus on today. What can we learn from the past? But in addition to that, what can we do to today? Can we change today? Today is an amazing gift that we have been given, and squandering it by focusing on the past is a habit we all need to break.

Change starts where you are today. Not yesterday, last month or last year, and it doesn't start tomorrow either. We have all made the excuses and pushed the start of a project to another day in the future. The most popular ones are, "I'll start on Monday," or "I'll start tomorrow," or maybe even, "I'll start on the first of the month." As I am writing this, New Year's is only a couple weeks away, which makes me think about everyone who puts off making changes or improvements to their lives until the new year rolls around. I am guilty of it too, so believe me, I am not picking on anyone here.

We always think there will be some sort of magical day or even this amazing starting-off point that will propel us into change. That somehow, tomorrow or the first of the year will be easier or different than all the other days we have available to us. We put it off because it is easier, too. The planning, the thinking, the plotting are easier than putting it into practice and actually starting the work.

But the truth is, while we are putting things off, we are wasting precious time that some are not even given. We fill our days with social media, television shows or social gatherings, and continue to put off change until some magical day in the future. The day comes, and once again we push it out and continue to hope while we waste more days in the process. Suddenly, a week, a month or a year goes by and that thing we so desperately want to achieve or do remains unchecked on our list of goals.

Change begins where you are right here and right now.

Your starting point is where you are in this place in time. Where you live, where you work, where you are with your health, finances, relationships, faith and every other area of your life. Like I said before, you cannot go back in time to start yesterday, and pushing it out until tomorrow is not doing you or I any favors. Today is where it is at. Today is where your power and control lie.

And the best way to begin your change today is to start small.

I have always been a big believer in drastic life changes or giving my existence a complete makeover in a short amount of time. I held onto that idea for years, until I realized that it never seemed to work. It took many, many attempts before I finally grasped that what I was doing was not working. I was expecting massive changes overnight, or I was hoping that after a short few days I would be thinking differently or my habits would be drastically improved. I would cram a bunch of new changes into my life, in several areas of my life, all at once and when it all came crashing down, I didn't recognize the reason for it. It never seemed to fully work, and I didn't understand what I was doing wrong.

I was making plans. I was putting in an effort. I was trying over and over again, doing things that mattered, that were good for me, and yet somehow, I wasn't getting anywhere.

I finally figured out that I was trying to do too much. As awesome as the thought of a complete overhaul life change was, I was trying to cram so many changes into my life at once that I was making it impossible for me to be successful. I was aiming high, which was great, but it was just too much for me to handle all at once. My focus was scattered, and I struggled to accomplish anything. No matter how hard I tried to change, it wouldn't work, and it just ended up being a disastrous mess I had to recover from.

Starting small is a great place to begin when you are trying to change the direction of your life, especially if you're seeking to alter a lot of aspects of your life like I always want to do. If your focus is on something more specific, then you can think a little bigger in terms of your steps to change. Sometimes when you start the process, you are not quite sure which direction you want to go or what you want to do. If you start the process of change with only a few things that need your attention, that allows you to take some time to think about what is next while making changes now. That way, you aren't wasting time while you begin the process.

One other great thing about starting small is that you save yourself from burning out too fast. As you can probably guess, part of the reason my big overall life-changing adventures didn't work was because of just that: I was doing so much that, eventually, it imploded and I lost the fire for what I was doing extremely fast. Don't get me wrong, every day isn't going to be an "on fire" day for you, and that is completely normal. But the overload that can come with changing too much too fast can cause you to flame out far more quickly and keep you from pressing forward for a long time. You can burn out and end up taking an extra-long time to start up again which, again, wastes your precious time.

Another great advantage is that you can get what Dave Ramsey refers to as a "quick win." When you are trying to change your financial situation, or any other part of your life, starting with smaller goals sets you up in a big way. Part of the *Financial Peace University* program is the idea of attacking your smallest debt first—a.k.a. the debt snowball. People always bring up the fact that if you pay off the debt with the highest interest rate first, you save yourself money. Although this is true, Dave's reason for saying a person should start with the smallest debt is because the process is a mental challenge, not a mathematical one.

If you set yourself up for a quick win, that, in turn, will help you build momentum and boost your confidence in the process. Getting quick wins is not just something you can use to improve your financial situation but rather can be applied to the rest of your life as well. It can help you build a business, or even create better relationships. It is a powerful thing that propels you forward to the goals you have for your life.

Right now, I want you to think about your life. We covered this a little bit in the introduction already, but I want this to be a continuation of that thought process. In fact, I am hoping that throughout the course of this book, you will continue to think about where your life is right now and where you want it to be. Thinking about the comparison between those two points is going to help you move forward and find some direction in this process. It will help you see what needs to be changed and what is working for you. Being able to step back and see where you are at point A and then where point B is will help you find the steps in between. And that is vital for any successful journey of change.

What are some areas of your life that need improving? Are you in a dead-end job that you dislike or are not terribly passionate about? Are you struggling with your health or wishing you were more fit? Are you deeply in debt or wish you had some more money to hold you over when things get tough? Is one of your relationships on the brink or do you desire to have someone special into your life? Are you wishing you were more educated, better at playing an instrument, or able to spend more time with your family? Those are only a few of the hundreds of questions I could be asking you right now, but hopefully, that gets your mind reeling a little.

We all have at least one area of our lives that is in need of improvement, in a big or small way. Maybe it is several areas of life that need change. Whatever your situation, we are all in this same place, one way or another. We are all in need of some change, improvements, and momentum forward into a better life.

Stop waiting for the perfect time or day. Right now, here, this moment, is all we have. Grab it with both hands and embrace the challenge.

Make a decision to move yourself toward a better life.

Chapter review:

Everyone has doubt, no matter how great their lives look on the outside.

The past is something we choose to hold onto—it is not holding onto us.

Focusing on the lessons you can learn from the past is the best way of letting things go and moving forward.

Starting small can stop you from burning out too fast.

Change starts where you are today! Not yesterday, not tomorrow.

Take action challenge!

It is challenge time!

What small steps can you take today to start improving your life? A few ideas would be adding a ten-minute walk to your morning, writing 500 words in the book you've always wanted to publish, reading a few pages of an inspiring book, eating some extra fruits or vegetables, or encouraging a friend. Sometimes it feels like changing our lives needs to be big and complicated, but the truth is it doesn't need to be. Take out a piece of paper and a pen right now and start brainstorming some ideas! What is something small you can do every day that will help you create the life you want?

Take action now!

Time is free, but it's priceless. You can't own it, but you can use it. You can't keep it, but you can spend it. Once you've lost it, you can never get it back.

~ Harvey MacKay

CHAPTER 2

UTILIZE TIME

It is amazing to think about how many times I have thought to myself, "I wish today would just be over already," or "If only it were tomorrow or the weekend, right now." I have wished time away. I have spent energy wishing the end of the workday would come, wanting an event I'm attending to be over with, or wishing the weekend would just come to an end already. Granted, that last one doesn't happen often, but we have all wished that a day, a week, or a month would just be over so we can get on to the next thing.

The trouble with that is we are failing to realize that today is where it is at. Today is where the power is, and wishing time away does us no good at all. In fact, it holds us back. Instead of using that time in some useful way, we are sitting on our hands waiting for that perfect day to show up and not using the time we are given to make some kind of impact, on our own lives or the lives of others.

One of my favorite quotes about the passing of time comes from a show that I love: *The Golden Girls*. (You may have laughed a little just now, which is fine with me. My love for

The Golden Girls remains!) This scene has played over and over in my mind so many times. Partly because it's hilarious, and partly because it holds a powerful truth.

The story starts out with Dorothy, Blanche, Rose, and Sophia crashing a high school reunion party. During the event, Rose had collapsed, but not before grabbing her arm and calling out for Dorothy.

The particular scene that I love in this storyline comes soon after. Dorothy, Blanche, and Sophia are seen standing around Rose, who is lying in a hospital bed. They are overjoyed because the doctor has said she is going to be okay. As they share their joy over the news, they begin to discuss what they want to do with their lives from here on out in appreciation for the time they have been given. Dorothy's response to Sophia's plan for the future is what many people's reaction would be, but Sophia's response to her is just pure gold.

> *Sophia: We've all gotten a second chance. I realized I wasn't living up to my potential. I'm gonna find out what I'm good at. Take an aptitude test. Maybe even go to law school.*
>
> *Dorothy: Oh, come on, Ma, you'll be 96 when you get out.*
>
> *Sophia: I'll be 96, anyway!*[3]

That scene never fails to crack me up. And it is such a great reminder that time will pass no matter what, and how much we utilize it is really up to us.

Sophia will be 96 anyway. The time will pass, whether she goes to law school or not, so why not do something meaningful with that time? Maybe law school doesn't quite make sense given her age, but on the same note, who says she couldn't do it? So now, let me ask you this question.

Who says you couldn't?

Maybe law school is not what you are looking to accomplish in your life, but I am guessing you have some burning desire inside of you that you would love to pursue. And the truth is, you can. You can use this time you have been given to take steps toward your goal. You can stop wishing and waiting for some magic to happen. You can make the magic. We each have the same number of hours in the day. We each have the same opportunity to use what time we are given to do something mediocre, something amazing, or nothing at all.

The choice is ours.

Yes, we all don't have the same family situation, the same job or the same relationship dynamics. Some people don't have others depending on them, don't have spouses to consult, or don't have children to take care of. And there are some who have busy calendars with school events and PTA meetings and work responsibilities during non-traditional business hours. What you have on your plate is not going to be the same as the person sitting next to you, your best friend or your boss. However, we all still have the same twenty-four hours in a day, and how we utilize them says a lot about how dedicated we are to the goals we have set for ourselves. If we are choosing activities during those hours that are either not benefiting our futures or just filling our minds with unimportant information, we are not going to achieve what we hope to.

Don't get me wrong here, relaxation and taking the time to decompress is essential. I am a big believer in recharging time and doing the things that help keep you functioning at your best. Taking the time to watch one of your favorite shows, read an awesome fiction book, or even get a little extra sleep are all great things when done here and there. However, making the powerful choice to use those extra minutes to squeeze in some personal development, some writing, some jumping jacks, or some financial planning is going to be more beneficial and a better use of your time in the long run.

Time is precious. Time moves whether you move or not. It continually presses on, forging ahead into the unknown whether you decide to join it or not. Time is a relentless bugger. It moves forward, second after second, and gives you the choice of whether or not you are going to utilize its true power.

Are you using your time the way you should? Are you doing what needs to be done?

I am not going to sit here and tell you I am perfect with my time. There are many days when I fail to do what needs to be done. I have put off my writing, my workouts, and my chores. I have chosen to disregard my financial goals and have spent time online shopping for things I don't need. I have failed to use my time wisely more times than I care to think about, but that is something that we can all improve upon.

One of my favorite books is *The Slight Edge* by Jeff Olson. It is definitely on my list of "must reads" for anyone who is looking to change their life. In his book, he talks about time and the power it has. I just love how he describes it:

Time is the force that magnifies those little, almost imperceptible, seemingly insignificant things you do every day into something titanic and unstoppable. You supply the actions; the universe will supply the time. The trick is to choose the actions that, when multiplied by this universal amplifier, will yield the result you want.[4]

Such true and powerful words.

I am sure you have heard the word "momentum." It is honestly one of my favorite words, especially on the subject of change. What am I talking about? Let's take a moment to define the word momentum so we can see how powerful it really is.

According to the dictionary, momentum is the "strength or force gained by motion or by a series of events."[5] It's like a snowball rolling down a hill. Not only does it grow, but it gets faster and faster. It would be like anything going down a hill, for that matter. As it falls, as it moves forward, it gains strength and speed, and obstacles that were once an issue no longer pose as big of a threat.

That can be your life.

Some common words for momentum are strength, force, power, drive, and propulsion. Think of how your life could expand in amazing ways by using these two tools; time and momentum. If you invested time in all the different areas of life you wanted to change, and the ones you want to improve or maintain, and then continually did those small things throughout your days, can you imagine how different your life would be? How amazing would it be? Maybe it is hard to see how because you are at the beginning of the journey, or maybe you've been on this journey before, but it has been so long that you have lost hope.

I understand how you could be skeptical. You might be thinking, *How in the world does this chick know my life could be any better or not? She hasn't walked in my shoes. She hasn't seen my family life, my job, my kids, or my bank account.*

You're right. I don't know. I have no idea where you are right now in your life. I don't know what your struggles are or what you are facing. I don't know what your hang-ups are, what derails you from chasing your goals or changing your life. I don't know what trials you have been through, and I am not going to pretend to know.

However, I do know this.

If you use time, if you build momentum, you can make changes to your life and change the outlook and outcome of your life. I know that for certain because I have done it myself.

I struggled a great deal with depression in my late teens and early twenties, but there was a time when I realized that I needed to change and start dealing with the things that were going on in my life. I also knew that this would not happen overnight. I knew that the changes I needed to make would not be easy and that I wouldn't wake up in a week all fixed. And, honestly, I am glad that didn't happen for me. Yes, it would be good to have things all nice and shiny, your life all fixed after making such a decision to change for the better, but the experience of fighting for a better life was one I needed. One I am truly grateful for.

Over time, life became easier to navigate. It was easier to walk away from bad friendships and easier to see roadblocks as opportunities. I learned what triggered downward spirals and how to retreat if I ended up in one. Learning these things took time; changing my direction took time. And understanding that it wouldn't be an overnight, magical fix made all the difference. I utilized the power of time to regain control of my life.

Momentum is powerful, but it requires you to start, to begin. If you choose to remain where you are and let time continue to pass without making an effort, you will continue to be a small snowball on the top of the hill. You will continue to be the same, or maybe even worse off, because you have failed to take steps forward. Momentum can and will only be utilized if you make a point to step forward and believe it is possible to change.

Momentum looks small at first. Its beginnings are so minute sometimes that you can hardly tell anything is happening. There is a change occurring, but you would need a microscope to see it or the effects of it. This is a frustrating place to be, but it is part of the process. If we can grasp that understanding, we are better off in the long run.

Weight loss is a great example. Do you want to lose 50 pounds? Let's do it. Well, you don't do that overnight. Trust me; I know that from personal experience. It happens over time. Over weeks and months and years, depending on how you approach it. Every pound lost is great, but for the first few weeks you feel like you are doing all of this work and nothing is showing up on the scale or your reflection doesn't seem to be any different. You feel discouraged and want to quit. If you do, you fail to see the power that momentum and time are having. But if you continue forward, one day you will realize how different you look, how baggier your clothes have become and how much more energy you have.

Because you have been utilizing the power of time and momentum, you have lost weight and gained strength, not to mention the drive to move forward having now seen the rewards of your efforts.

What is more motivational than that?

It is a matter of understanding that each decision, each step forward, adds up to big results. Making the most of the time you have and choosing to do what needs to be done to gain momentum (even when you can't see it) get you closer to the life you've always wanted. Most of the great things in life happen this way, and not by lightning strikes like winning the lottery. This is how success is found and built. However you define success, this is how you make it happen.

The small things add up to big things. It is just a matter of being intentional and using your time to do those small things, continually doing them to build momentum, and being patient for the results to show themselves.

Life doesn't change instantly like we sometimes hope it would. I can't eat well one day and expect to be at my goal weight the next day. It sure would be nice, but unfortunately, it doesn't work that way. I can't save money one day and expect to have a million dollars the next day. That just isn't realistic. Just like any success someone might have, change is built over days, weeks, months and years. It would be so nice to put in a little effort and wake up healthier, wealthier and more fulfilled. Yet we cannot cling to that thought or hope because it will get in the way of what makes life change for the better: time and momentum.

We get so many things instantly these days, and that list gets longer and longer every day as new technology comes into our lives. We get food faster, music faster, basically anything we want to purchase we can find somewhere online. Working toward something and waiting for the results to arrive is not something that comes naturally to us anymore. Maybe it never did, but now it is even harder to grasp that idea because of the instant world we live in.

But the truth is that most of the greats and geniuses, the successful CEO's and entrepreneurs, the people who have millions of dollars or financial freedom, did not get there in an instant. They did not reach their status overnight. They worked for it. They put time into it. And they let momentum work for them. Instead of their successes happening in an instant, it happened because of a lot of little instances, compounded over time.

They researched their interest and discussed the subject with others in the same field. They spent time testing out ideas, failing and then testing them out again. Tweaking projects, testing theories, asking for opinions, asking for advice. Over and over and over again, over the years many times, and they finally achieve what they had been working toward. They look like an overnight success to us only because we see the end result of their efforts. In reality, they have been putting in hours of work over the years to find their way to their goals, their dreams.

I am sure you have heard of the 10,000-hour rule, but sometimes it is good to remind ourselves of what it takes to get to what we see as success in the world today. The 10,000-hour rule is a principle, popularized by writer

Malcolm Gladwell, which says that 10,000 hours of focused effort is what you need to invest to become successful in your particular field of study or interest. So, according to Gladwell, if you want to be a successful writer, musician, doctor, mechanic, or whatever your field of interest may be, to get to a high level of success you must put in a great deal work. There are arguments against this rule, but Gladwell has made a point of reminding readers that there is an investment of time required for natural ability to manifest success.[6]

In this day and age, with everything that is at our fingertips, you could definitely get there much quicker. But no matter how many hours you are putting in, there is still effort, time and momentum required. You still aren't getting there overnight.

Focusing our energy on the things that can get us closer to our goals is going to do us a lot more good than spending time on actions that make us look busy but in fact waste time. We all do it; I'm just as guilty of it. It is easy to get stuck in a cycle of certain activities that make us look and feel busy but don't move us any closer to where we want to go. Identifying these activities in our lives can actually wake us up to what is important and makes a difference. For example, I can find myself getting caught up in planning sometimes. I love the planning process so much, but without action, it is kind of pointless. Planning without action is a waste of my time and energy. I would be better off doing something else if I am not going to carry out the plans I create.

We all have something that wastes our time, keeps us busy and away from doing the things that make an impact on our lives. Sometimes it is something that seems productive but isn't. Sometimes it's an excessive amount of time associated with a hobby or activity that we enjoy but doesn't add value to our lives. Identifying these things is going to help you get out of your own way and help you take more steps forward to your goals.

What we need to start realizing, myself included, is that time and momentum are our friends. They are our allies, really. Like compound interest, time and momentum seem insignificant until all our little steps, our decisions, our choices, our efforts are laid out, one after the other. They seem so small at the time, but suddenly you look back and see all the work you have done. All of the effort you have put in. And you realize that you have created a new life for yourself. You have changed your home life, your career path, or your relationships. You have changed your health, the amount of money in your bank account, or the amount of debt you have. You have become more knowledgeable or better at a specific skill you are interested in.

And all because you embraced time, momentum, and today. And every "today" you had after that.

I have heard the saying "today is all we have," so many times in my life. I never really thought much of it, but I have learned how true it is. I am a planner and a scheduler. I am sure you will see that throughout this book over and over again because it is something that is engrained so deeply into me for whatever reason. I love looking ahead, and it is important to do that. Having something to aim for or look forward to is a big deal. It gets us excited and moving. It wakes us up in the morning and keeps us motivated to keep trying to continually improve.

However, embracing the day we have in front of us is where the power is. Today is the day we have control over, for the most part. Yes, there are things we cannot control, and we will talk about some of that later, but most of the time there are things we can do, change, alter or refocus. We cannot do it tomorrow; we can only do that today. We can put it off until tomorrow, for sure, but it doesn't help us where we are at right now. It doesn't forward our position or get us closer to change faster.

Today is where our power and control are. We have a choice in how we want to use it, how we focus our energy, how we embrace what is in front of us and how we use it to our advantage. The next twenty-four hours is where our focus should be, keeping our end goals in mind, but focusing on right here and now. What can we do differently? What can we do better? Is there anything that we need to change our attitude about in order to keep our focus on what is important? How can we influence the situation and the people around us for the better? How can we embrace today in ways we never have before to get us closer to changing our lives in big ways?

When we embrace today and keep our allies of time and momentum close by, we have the chance—the opportunity—to change our lives in huge ways. And as a result, improve the lives of those around us. In the end, isn't that what we all want to do?

Time is your ally, and I hope you realize that. I hope you can see that it is something that can work for you in order to get closer to your goals. Time moves forward, so make an effort and move forward with it.

You won't regret it!

Chapter review:

Stop wishing and waiting for some magic to happen. You can make the magic.

We each have the same opportunity to use what time we are given to do something mediocre, something amazing, or nothing at all.

Time moves forward, whether you do or not.

The way you utilize your time says a lot about how dedicated you are to the goals you have set for yourself.

If you use time, if you build momentum, you can make changes to your life and change the outlook and outcome of your life.

Momentum can only be utilized if you make a point to step forward and believe it is possible to change.

Take action challenge!

Are you ready for a challenge? Let's do this!

As we have discussed, utilizing your time is a major step in changing your life. So let me ask you, are you utilizing yours? Take a minute right now to think about your day and how you structure it. Are you making the most of your time in order to get closer to your goals? Could you use your lunch hour differently? Could you arrive earlier, or stay a little later? Could you give up one of your favorite TV shows or cut back on a certain hobby in order to take a step forward to creating a better life for yourself?

What could you do to utilize your time better starting today?

Take action now!

At some point you just have to let go of what you thought should happen and live in what is happening.

~ Heather Hepler

CHAPTER 3

LIFE HAPPENS

Let's face it: things change, people change, and situations change. While we are on our journey to improving our lives and that of our families, the world around us is changing, and the people in it as well. As frustrating as that might be at times, it is something we have to take into account when it comes to pursuing our goals. It is one of those things that we have to take stock of from time to time and be willing to adjust what we are doing because of it.

Over the next couple chapters, we are going to cover a great deal that has to do with this topic because, let's face it, life happens, and it happens often. If I could plan out my life for the next ten years, I probably would. I have set up so many plans myself in the past but haven't accounted for the unknown as much as I should have. I wasn't ready for it, I should say. And when some life-altering event happened, my plan just became garbage in my mind, and I gave up on what I was working toward because something happened that I wasn't expecting.

Instead of being mentally ready for the possibility of my plans being interrupted, I ended up blindsided and derailed because I had forgotten one key thing about living.

Life is fluid.

Life changes so much, and sometimes it feels like it is happening out of the blue. There are times when we are lucky enough to see the changes coming ahead of time, and we can plan for them. We can prepare ourselves and adjust our minds to be ready for what is coming.

Unfortunately, most of the time it doesn't work out that way. Someone we love more than anything passes away, and suddenly we are left with a whole new existence to get used to without them. Our plans to improve and change ourselves become less important or less of a focus. And understandably so. The same would be true with the loss of a job and going from no great financial concerns to a great deal of worry over how you are going to deal with this new situation. Wondering how you are going to provide for your family and considering the possibilities, both good and bad. Once again, our plans to improve and change ourselves become less important or less of a focus for us. And once again, that is understandable.

My question is, how long do we linger there? How long do we remain in this space of doing nothing, changing nothing, and facing nothing? Every situation is different, and I am not going to sit here and tell you how long you should mourn or how long you should worry about finding employment. I can't do that and wouldn't be bold enough to make any assumptions there. What I do want to challenge you on is how long you give up on improving your life. Maybe you need to readjust things, which we will talk about later, but for now, perhaps you need to focus on half of what you set out to do. Maybe a few things on your list aren't relevant anymore because your situation changed.

The point is, I don't want you to give up on changing or improving your life when obstacles hit you out of the blue. In extreme cases, taking a break and re-evaluating is a great thing to do. But remaining on the sidelines for too long will only hold you back from achieving your best, and you would be depriving the world of the best you. I don't want that to happen.

Other life changes to consider would be a change in a relationship. There are different levels here, and some are more involved than others. You may be newly married, or just getting a divorce after twenty years. You may be just starting to date or have been in a long-term relationship and have just broken up. Wherever you are on that spectrum, there is change involved. You are either gaining or losing. And when that happens, your life takes on a new color, a new focus. You either spend more time alone or now your time involves or revolves around another person. Life changes.

I don't know the ins and outs of relationships, especially ones that have been in existence for several years; I haven't gotten that far myself. But I have seen relationships fall apart after a long period of time and watched the people in the situation try to find themselves again. One thing I have noticed from watching couples go through tough times is that the ones who come out of it on the other side as better people, either together or apart, are the ones who focus on improving themselves, learning from their mistakes and investing time into becoming better people.

Instead of being 100 percent the victim in the situation, they figure out what they did wrong, what they could have done differently, and what they will do from now on and in the process of healing. Together or apart, they discover new things about themselves and don't spend all their energy for the rest of their lives wallowing in grief. They do allow themselves to feel the pain and the hurt, as they should.

My point is, they don't get trapped there.

It is easy to focus our energy on the struggle and who we can blame. We want to tell people about how we were wronged and how the other person was so awful for doing what they did. There are so many different scenarios I could list here, but I don't want to focus on that.

Life will happen to you; one way or another, it happens to all of us. Something good will happen, something bad will happen. Most of the time we can't prepare for it. However, we can prepare ourselves by embracing this truth.

Life will throw a curveball, and we have the power to choose how to move forward in our new circumstances. We can live in a cycle of victimhood, or we can take a step back, reevaluate and move forward.

It is our choice.

As I am writing this, I keep thinking about when I was living out in Portland and broke my toe. Life happened, and given the situation I was in, my options were limited. I was working two jobs in two different towns, living in a third-floor apartment with no elevator and not allowed to use stairs or carry more than a certain amount of weight, which meant getting groceries was anything but easy. To get down the stairway, I would slide down two flights on my rear end, and to get back up to my apartment I would crawl on my hands and knees up the stairs. Not a pretty sight, I am sure. To add insult to injury, I wasn't in a situation where I could handle it financially, and I didn't have anywhere I could crash for the next three months while I healed.

It was a bit of a mess. Life happened.

It was hard for me, and I did do my fair share of wallowing, especially when I made the decision to move back to Minnesota and give up my life in Oregon after only six short but glorious months. Just thinking about it now makes my heart jump into my throat. I had dreamed of living in Portland for so long, and my time there was cut short. But at that moment in time, I didn't have a choice. My options were few, and I had to suck it up, give up a lot of my stuff including my car, and hop (on crutches) on the train back to the Midwest.

It was a tough decision to make, but given the circumstances, it was the best choice. It would have been a long and tough few months if I would have tried to stay in Oregon. Was it my dream to be there? Yes. But my situation had changed. I was no longer in a position to take care of myself. The simplest things were extremely difficult and taxing to carry out, mentally and physically. Leaving was hard, but how could I have survived three months or more given the situation?

Life had changed and as difficult as it was to do, I had to change my plans along with it. It was hard to have a good attitude about it as I agonized over the choices that I had in front of me, but in the end, I knew it was best given all the information I had at that point. Going home was my best bet if I wanted to heal quickly, and heal correctly, for that matter. I wanted to do what was right for my healing process, so I went back home.

Sometimes the changes that are happening in life are actually happening to another person or people you know, but it affects you in some way. Somehow your life overlaps with theirs, and suddenly you are in the mix of something that doesn't have a lot to do with you. Those situations can be hard and can test a person's patience. You don't know when to step away, when to offer help, or when to give advice. Those situations can feel like a trap at times. You want to get away from it, but it isn't as easy as walking away.

When someone else has changes in their life that seem to seep into yours, you have to take stock and do it often. When you are connected to someone else's drama, it can suck the life out of you and begin to become a burden. You're always there, around it, hearing things, seeing things, but maybe not in a position to do much about it at all, which only adds to the frustration. You want things to improve, you want to escape, and you feel trapped.

Taking stock during these times is crucial because it allows you to see the truth. If you can take a step back and see what is going on, what power you do or don't have, you will be able to continue to move forward. Because the truth is, in most cases, you do have some options. You may find yourself in a place that is full of negativity, which starts to find its way into other areas of your life. Fortunately, you have the power to not let that happen. You don't have to let the misery, the angst, and the drama become yours and stop you from living your best life.

If you don't have a way to move forward because of this situation you are connected to, you are responsible for finding a way. Whether that means leaving where you are, putting up boundaries between you and others or maybe even cutting ties with the individuals that are causing you to lose focus and pulling you into their drama. Sometimes that needs to happen in order for you to be able to take care of yourself and not let it affect the rest of your life. It isn't an easy thing to do, but there are times when it is necessary. And though the change could be challenging, in the end, you find yourself in a better place. Physically, perhaps, but what I am really referring to here is finding yourself in a better mental place, a better headspace.

Don't let other's drama change who you are and what you are. Help them if you can. Encourage them. Love on them. Be with them. I don't want to say you or anyone else should cut people from your lives because of drama, because, let's face it, we have our fair share. (And anyone who says they don't have drama doesn't know themselves very well, in my opinion anyway.) The important thing is not letting yourself become a victim of the tornado, especially if they are unwilling to help or change themselves. That right there, my friends, is a giant red flag. That is what I want you to steer clear of, or at the very least cut down on your connection to. Inviting others' problems into your life is a part of being a friend. We carry each other's burdens as we walk through life. It is hard sometimes, but it is awesome to have connections like that with people.

But if the person is continually the victim, is continuously involved in and creating drama, and is refusing to make changes that could help them move forward, after a while that is going to burn you out and start affecting your life, your plans, your responsibilities. That is not a fair trade. Love them, care for them, but put up boundaries.

Another thing I want you to remember is that when things change, and the unexpected happens, you shouldn't hold your feelings in. I am giving you permission to let them out. Be respectful if you are dealing with another person, of course. I don't want to sound like I am giving you permission to go off on someone and treat others in a disrespectful way. Please don't do that.

The truth is, acting like things are fine and not dealing with the emotions that come with whatever is going on in your life isn't healthy either. It can build up over time and come out in other ways. You can hold it in now and end up taking it out on someone else. It can bubble up at an inappropriate and inconvenient time. Has that ever happened to you?

I have been there a few times, fuming inside my own head over something that happened and then treating someone disrespectfully as a result, even when it wasn't their fault. Or I snap or use a tone of voice that is unjustified. It slips out sometimes, but it is a matter of not letting it come to that. It's important to deal with the situation and the feelings that come along with them as they happen, rather than letting them build up. You'll be happy you did in the end, and those who you share your life with will be glad you did as well.

Life changes, every single day. Sometimes in big ways, sometimes in little ways we hardly notice, but it is a constant state of being. And once we hold onto that truth, once we embrace the fact that one of the only constants in life is that things change, we hold the power to face those changes as they come. They may hurt for a while, they may leave scars, but they don't have to derail our futures. They don't have to uproot us from our plans. They don't have to completely distract us from the goals we have for our lives and the ways we want to impact those around us.

They don't have to. And how do we avoid letting these situations take us down? We prepare ourselves for what is true. We embrace the understanding that life is ever changing, ever moving, and we don't let ourselves fall off track every time life throws us a curveball.

Will we fall off track from time to time? Yes. Sometimes getting off the track is necessary while you reevaluate things. As we have discussed, there are circumstances where this makes sense. But don't let these curveballs take you out of the game entirely. You are capable of powering through the changes that are happening.

Sometimes when unexpected things happen, it is important to ask yourself some questions, such as, why did I start on this journey? Or why do I want to make this particular change? What is it I am hoping to accomplish? What will my life look like once this goal is completed? It is important to pose these questions when you begin to get off track. In fact, ask them right now, write down the answers and put them in a place you will see them often, like the refrigerator door or your bathroom mirror. The time will come when you hit a rough patch, and when you do, you can revert back to these answers, find your footing again and move forward.

Life happens to the best and worst of us. In other words, all of us. If things don't go our way, it is hard to deal with sometimes, but that is how life is. We have the choice of what we want to focus on and where we are going to put our energy. We have the choice in how we are going to react and ultimately live out our lives.

Please understand that a curveball is coming. I can't tell you when or how or who will be involved. I can't tell you if it is big or small or if it will make you laugh or cry. Do your best to be prepared for it and when it comes, don't let it get you off track. Don't let it change the course of your future. Don't let it force you to stop trying to evolve and grow as a person.

Keep pushing forward.

Chapter review:

Sometimes taking a break from your mission of change is vital when your life situation changes; however, remaining on the sidelines for too long will only hold you back from achieving your goals.

Life will throw curveballs at you, but you choose how you are going to move forward in your new circumstances.

Taking stock during these times of changes in your life is crucial because it allows you to see the truth and what options and choices you actually have.

When unexpected things happen in life, it is important to deal with the feelings you have that come along with them as they happen, rather than letting them build up.

You have the choice of what you want to focus on and where you're going to put your energy.

Take action challenge!

Challenge time!

Have you had any new changes in your life? Has life blindsided you recently? Maybe it is time to take stock of where you are and what your priorities need to be. It is so easy to get distracted from your goals when something changes unexpectedly. Do you need to take a break from your goals to reassess? Or have you been on the sidelines for a while and need to get back to work on your goals?

Take a moment to think about your current situation and decide what your next move needs to be.

Take action now!

I can't change the direction of the wind, but I can adjust my sails to always reach my destination.

~ Jimmy Dean

CHAPTER 4

DYNAMIC PLANS

In the last chapter, we talked a little bit about how life changes. That there are times when we are blindsided and have to deal with life events we never saw coming. The truth is life will change, and that is something we can count on. And we can be assured it will happen often and when we least expect it.

Because of this truth in our lives, we need to be flexible with how we chase our goals and make our plans. There has to be an element of flexibility and mobility that goes along with what we are hoping to accomplish. I think I said this in the last chapter, but I'll say it again. I don't like it when plans change. If I could plan out the next ten years of my life, I probably would. The element of control is what I always want. I love it when I know what is going to happen and how I am going to deal with things when they do occur. I am one of those people who work through every scenario you can possibly think of when I am preparing for certain situations or life changes. If I am facing something new or something I haven't had to deal with in a long time, I try to come at it from every angle to get myself ready for whatever is ahead of me.

I know it's crazy, but I like to plan for the unplanned.

It is exhausting at times, but my mind goes there every time. It is like I am trying to prepare myself for things going wrong. Or not going my way, I suppose. Most of the time, planning for various scenarios ends up being unnecessary, but I go there every time no matter what.

When it comes to plans, we have to be ready for those life changes in some aspect. We have to at least be ready with the knowledge that something will happen, big or small, and it won't always be something we can prepare for, unfortunately. (You have no idea how much I don't like that last part.) We may not have a set plan for the unplanned, but having the knowledge that change is coming is powerful.

When it comes to chasing goals and changing your life, being willing to adjust your plans as life changes is going to help you go so much further. It is hard for me to admit that, believe me, but it is the truth, and I feel like I have learned that over and over again. I love planning, and I love what it entails. I tend to put lots of work into my plans, so when something happens that ultimately forces me to adjust my course, my first instinct is to resist it. I don't want to give up on my plan; I don't want to change what I am doing. It looks good on paper and would be so beautiful in reality, so why can't I just continue down this road?

Sometimes it takes some pulling and tugging, and maybe a few shed tears before I'm willing to let go of my original plan, because I'm kind of stubborn. At some point, I finally realize that I need to change my plan in order to move forward.

Plans for change should be as dynamic as life is.

When you have your heart set on something, when you have certain expectations, or when you have hopes of achieving a specific goal that is precious to your heart, being forced to rethink those things can be difficult to do. It can be a hard thing to face up to. We want to stay on this particular road to this specific destination, but sometimes it doesn't work out that way. I say sometimes, but I should say often because the reality is that what gets us to our goals, what gets us the life we want, is often something we haven't considered or figured into our plan.

Often the detours we take in life can propel us forward into achieving the things we hoped to achieve and much more we never dreamed of.

For me, moving back to the Midwest wasn't in my grand plan when I left for Portland in the summer of 2014. I was going to move west and work, begin writing and build a whole new life for myself out there. Well, God had other plans and seemed to lead me back here. I didn't understand it. Sometimes it was easy to deal with; sometimes I was wallowing in grief over it. It took me a while to find my footing, but because of my experience of leaving home, I had rediscovered myself in many ways. Being away from home like that, living in a place I hardly knew in a neighborhood I had never been to, was such a great experience, and I realized when I came back that I was not the same person anymore. A short six months out there changed me.

Even though returning to Minnesota wasn't easy for me, what I gained during my time away and the adjustment back to life at home was monumental to me. I no longer felt like I had to live in a box that others had put me in or one I had put myself in. I didn't have to live a certain expected life just because it was what everyone else was doing. I could pursue my goals here or there; the location wasn't the issue.

I was the issue.

My plan had to change because my circumstances had changed. I needed to go with the flow instead of fighting against it or acting like a victim. I needed to face my new life in an old location and not dwell on the fact that part of my dream was cut short. I realized that the dreams I had could happen here, too. I had to change my plan; I had to adjust my thinking.

Another thing to consider here is timing. Maybe it wasn't time for me to be out there permanently. Maybe I needed this adjustment in order to spark something inside of me to change. Sometimes when life throws us a curveball, it isn't meant to destroy us but to wake us up or get us unstuck. It may be meant to shake up the way we are thinking or maybe force our hand and make us head in a better direction. Leaving where I had wanted to live since I was sixteen years old was very difficult. Looking back, though, I realize that even though my time there was short, it was precisely what I needed to propel my life forward, to change me for the better, and to give me a new outlook on life. I see life through a different lens than I did before. It is a gift I was given, and I will forever be grateful for that.

Will I end up moving back west at some point? That remains to be seen, but I do know that adjusting my plan, and being flexible with life, is what will help me get back to the West Coast, bring me to a different location, or keep me in Minnesota. No matter where I end up, I am going to thrive.

When it comes to this topic of plans being dynamic, I think it is important to discuss failure as well. We will cover this more throughout the next few chapters here and there, so don't be surprised if it pops up again, but failure is something we all identify with in some way. We could be truly failing at something, but more than likely we are pegging ourselves as failures when indeed we are not. I struggle with this one myself. It is so easy to define a situation in a way that makes you believe to your core that you have failed. That somehow you have messed up so badly that your life is just one big mistake. Whether you are very dramatic about it or only semi-convinced of it, failure is something we all cling to in some way. We assume the worst of ourselves, of others, or of situations. This happens especially when we are unable to step outside ourselves and see things from different angles.

There is also this element of feeling like a failure if we have to detach or change our plans. "This didn't go the way I had planned so, obviously, I am a failure." I understand the feeling, but oftentimes, it isn't the truth. Not even close to the truth, though it sure feels like it is. Having to give up on a dream you've held close for years, whether temporarily or permanently, is painful. There are no two ways about it. Having to say, "This isn't working anymore like I had hoped it would and now I have to walk away," isn't an easy thing to do. However, sometimes it is the best thing we can do for ourselves.

Failure, or the presumption of it, is a horrible feeling. It is like one of those aching pains in our minds or hearts that just never wants to leave. The sense of failure is a burden we can carry, and it can influence our decisions, our attitude and everything in between. I don't like living moments, hours, days or weeks feeling that what I am doing is somehow a huge mistake.

I should ask you, how do you define failure? Sometimes I believe we skew it in our minds to mean something other than what it means. Or we apply it to ourselves or our lives in ways that don't quite fit, but we convince ourselves that it makes perfect sense.

One of my favorite definitions of failure is as follows: failure is the lack of success.[7]

Why is this my favorite definition? Because how we define success for ourselves ultimately triggers how we define our failures. That right there is powerful.

One of my best friends and I had a conversation about a year ago that I will never forget. I was struggling to find some direction in my life, and I felt like such a loser. I would set these big goals and find myself going other directions and not following through because it just didn't feel like it was right for me anymore or something had happened to redirect me. Even though most of the time, my choice in changing my focus had merit and reasons behind it, it made me feel like I was failing. But, as usual, my friend set me straight.

"You only lose [fail] when you stop searching, stop going for stuff, stop reaching." And she was right. (She usually is.)

I had defined success as hitting specific goals, no matter what. If I didn't accomplish something I set out to do, I labeled myself as a failure, even if pursuing that goal didn't make any sense anymore. I said I would do it, so I should do it, no matter what. That is ridiculous.

Failure happens when a person continues to do things that don't work or when they choose not to adjust to the events that happen in their life. It happens when they choose to focus more on the results they have or haven't achieved over the effort they are putting in. When you stop trying, stop growing, stop learning and stop pushing forward to build a better life for yourself and your family, that is when failure comes into play. Even when you fall short of your goals, that doesn't make you a failure. You may have failed to hit a target, but you only fail if you choose not to figure out how you can grow and learn from the experience.

Sometimes when our plans change, when life throws us a curveball, we may not know what to do with it. We may not know how to handle it or how to move forward because of it. This is one of those moments when you need to ask for help. I know, you might be like me and struggle with the thought of inviting someone else into the situation. Asking for help isn't easy for me, so if you struggle with it too, I feel your pain. The need for help sometimes makes me feel like I'm not strong enough or capable enough to handle a situation. It makes me feel like I'm needy and not independent.

The truth is that asking for help when you need it most, or just when you need it period, is a sign of strength of character. It is also proof that you are human. Asking someone to help you through a change gives you a chance to learn humility and allows another person to be of service to you. Isn't that one of our duties as friends? As family? To assist those we love through tough times and periods of adjustment? You've helped them; it is okay to ask them to help you.

Sometimes the changes in our plans don't require major assistance, but allowing someone into the situation and letting them speak into how you could handle what is going on, how you could view it, is a great thing for both sides. Don't be too stubborn to ask for help when you need it. And yes, that last sentence was for myself as well. It is easy to be stubborn. It is easy to keep people at a distance when things are complicated or up in the air, wanting to tackle these issues on our own and not be a burden on others. Sometimes you need another set of eyes on what is going on in your life, and that is a beautiful thing.

When your life changes and your plans need to be adjusted, resist the urge to fight it. Don't waste your time and energy battling the fact that the plan you created doesn't fit your life anymore, because that is exactly what is going on. Your life outgrew your plan in some way. You were headed boldly in one direction, and now you are headed in another. That is what happens in life, and that is how life is always going to be, so don't fight the fact that your plans need to change from time to time. The longer you fight the inevitable, meaning the longer you fight the fact that change happens in life, the longer you are putting off valuable opportunities and personal growth. You are putting off chances to get closer to your goals. Don't do that to yourself; it isn't worth the energy.

Accept the change—embrace it, in fact—and move forward. Don't fight it; adjust with it.

When your plans need to change, take the time to acknowledge how it makes you feel. Understanding and identifying the emotions you are having about what is happening is necessary. Don't bottle up your frustrations. Don't pretend you are fine with it when you aren't. Once again, don't wallow here, but it is important to identify what is going on in your mind and how this need to adjust your plan is affecting you. When that curveball comes, we all react in different ways, and allowing ourselves to feel our feelings is something I believe we all need. This does not give you permission to take things out on the people around you, but it gives you the go-ahead to acknowledge your feelings.

When I was laid off from my job before moving west, I could have lashed out. I was hurt by their decision to let me go, but I also understood that at that time, they needed to let some people go and I happened to be one of them. The layoff wasn't personal, but I allowed myself to grieve the loss. I cried, I screamed, and I vented. And then I began to dream about what I could do next.

This life event ultimately led to the opportunity and decision to head west. If I wouldn't have been laid off, I may have never left Minnesota. And without that move, I wouldn't have experienced and learned everything that I did.

It isn't always enjoyable at the time when you are forced to adjust to the changes that life brings, but later on, we can look back and see the beauty in what took place. Control what you can: your attitude, your reaction, your work ethic, your effort, and your investments into your life. You can control that. And as plans change, know that this change, whether it is good or bad, will bring you opportunities for growth. You just have to be open to the idea.

The truth of the matter is that change is an opportunity. When something bad happens, or when something great happens, change is a chance for us all to grow and learn. It is a chance for us to become better at the things we love or find new things to enjoy and aim for. Change can be hard, it can be frustrating, especially when we have set out this whole plan for our lives that to us is perfect and everything we've ever wanted. Just remember that when our plans need to change, we are being given a gift, even if we can't see it at the time.

Embrace the gift of change and adjust your plans. Because life is dynamic.

Chapter review:

Being willing to adjust your plans as your life changes is going to help you go so much further.

Often the detours we take in life can propel us forward into achieving the things we hoped to achieve and much more we never dreamed of.

How you define success for yourself ultimately triggers how you define failures.

Don't waste your time and energy battling the fact that the plan you created doesn't fit your life anymore.

When something bad happens, or when something great happens, change is a chance for us all to grow and learn.

Take action challenge!

Challenge time! Gear up!

So, we have just discussed how plans need to be dynamic because life is ever changing. Have you hit a point where your plans to move forward don't seem to make sense anymore? What has recently changed that is causing you to question your current path? And one more question. Are you fighting to hold onto a plan that needs to be changed or abandoned for a new one? I know how hard it is to adjust your goals and plans when unexpected things happen, but I challenge you to take time right now to think about these questions and answer them for yourself.

Don't get stuck in a loop and hold onto things that aren't working.

Take action now!

Life is ten percent what happens to you and ninety percent how you react to it.

~ Charles Swindoll

CHAPTER 5

CHOOSE YOUR ATTITUDE

When you begin the process of making changes in your life, your attitude is one of the most important tools you have at your disposal. How you view the world, your situation, your relationships, and your life all come into play when you are trying to change your present reality. I want us to dive into this for a full chapter because I believe it so deeply. I want you to begin to really understand and see how much your outlook affects the things you say you want to accomplish and how to harness your attitude to create a great life for yourself and those you care about.

You've probably heard someone say that attitude is everything. Well, I don't know if it is everything or not, but I do believe—no, I know—it is a powerful thing that can propel you forward. Or, it can hold you back.

What it does is really up to you.

We are all born with different personalities. We are all unique individuals, which is a beautiful thing. Some of my best friends are so different than me. One friend is on the opposite end of the spectrum in almost every way, but she remains one of my closest friends. (And you're stuck with me forever, twit! Don't ever forget that!) We all come with a different set of mental tools, I guess you could say. Some people are very extroverted. Some are very introverted. And then there are those of us that fall somewhere in the middle of the spectrum. When it comes to being introverted or extroverted, there isn't a bad side to be on. The point is, we all have different strengths and different weaknesses. We all have various ways of facing situations and dealing with people.

We all come wired differently, and, because of that, we need to acknowledge that we do not face the things that come into our lives the same way. However, we cannot use the differences we have to excuse ourselves from being responsible for how we use what we are given. And we should not avoid personal growth in the areas that we struggle in either, because that is just one big cop-out.

As I am typing this, I keep thinking about this gentleman whom I met at a job I had. He had been there for years before I showed up at the company, and his attitude always struck me as pretty awful. He was always negative, regardless of what was going on. There was always a storm cloud over him even when everyone else was admiring the sunshine and blue skies. No matter what you said to him, he would always come back with a complaint or an issue he had with the work or someone he was working with.

Each conversation I had with him became shorter every time because I couldn't handle his attitude. I held onto my cheerful outlook when we exchanged words, but it wasn't easy. After a while, I tried to avoid him if I could. I did my best not to be rude and tried to be kind, but his raincloud attitude was frustrating to deal with on a regular basis.

I remember someone saying, "That's just how he is. That's just who he is." And of course, in my head I would be asking, *why?* Why was he like that, every single day? My best guess was that his life had been hard, that he had gone through a great deal of struggle in his life. There was a giant chip on his shoulder you couldn't get off without a sandblaster and about twenty-four hours of pressure on it. I believe people are influenced and affected by the experiences they have in their lives. I am a product of my own, just like you are and he is. However, our attitude determines where that can take us.

We can be victims, or we can be victors.

I don't know about you, but I want to be a victor in my own life. I hope that is what you want as well, for yourself and those around you. I want to rise above the hard situations. I want to achieve what I set out to do. I don't want to spend my life whining about every little thing that goes wrong because, frankly, there is always going to be something going wrong. Something little, something big. It happens. It is another one of the guarantees of life. Life changes, things go wrong.

But we don't have to focus on that either; that is my point. We can prepare ourselves for it, maybe only with the knowledge that the possibility is out there, but we don't have to focus on it. Our attention doesn't have to be on everything that has gone wrong or will go wrong. The past isn't always the most enjoyable thing to focus on, and focusing on all the possibilities of disaster ahead? That can torture a person.

I am guilty of both, in all honesty. I've tortured myself from both sides, which I am sure isn't an uncommon thing. (Please agree with me so that I won't feel so crazy.) It is easy to get caught up in what could have been or what might be. It is hard not to go there, but pulling ourselves from that vicious cycle can save us from a lot of pain and grief in the future.

I don't know what happened in this guy's life, or what hardships he faced. I could speculate, but that would be a waste of our time. The truth is, he still had a choice to treat people with dignity and respect. He wouldn't have to be a nonstop ray of sunshine or anything. He wouldn't have to come into work singing and laughing. But he could be kind, courteous and thankful. I always wonder how his life could be different if he were to choose a better attitude. He might get more recognition. He might get a raise. He might find a friend.

Which brings up another point about our attitude: it is not only a tool that can be used in the process of changing your life, but it can also attract allies that could help you get there faster. Suddenly, your journey isn't a solo one but a group effort, as you both (or all) move forward. I don't know about you, but people who have a decent outlook on life are the ones I gravitate toward and want to be friends with. Yes, there are varying degrees of optimism, but the ones who aren't constantly in their cloud of misery or aren't complaining all the time, those are the people I want to be around.

Treating others like he did kept people at a distance. His attitude and demeanor may have been a safety mechanism on his part, to keep people away because he has been hurt in the past. We have all been there before ourselves, but in the end, we lose out on valuable friendships and relationships if we keep people at arm's length all the time. We need other people. He needs other people. And our attitudes can keep the people we might truly need in our lives from ever getting close to us.

We all have our moments. I am not expecting everyone to be giddy and happy all the time, because that would be an unrealistic standard no one could live up to. Nevertheless, seeing the positive in situations and treating people right is a choice. You could be having the worst day ever, however you would define that for yourself, but that doesn't give you the right to treat people in a disrespectful way. People might excuse it for you, or you might excuse it yourself, but your circumstances do not have to determine your outlook on every area of your life. And they do not have to determine how you treat people.

You have the power; you have the choice.

Your attitude not only attracts people into (or repels people from) your life, it also attracts (or repels) opportunities. It is weird how this works sometimes, but what you put out there you seem to get back. When you are both working toward something and choosing the right attitude about it, somehow that multiplies in other areas of your life.

Your attitude is so powerful that it can propel you forward or backward. There is no standing still; you are going one direction or the other. Your attitude of victim or victor is your ally, so it is important to choose wisely.

Choosing your action and reaction is something we should discuss here as well because it goes along the same lines as your attitude. Just like our attitudes, we have a choice in how we act and how we react. We may have natural inclinations to do one thing or another, to say one thing or another, but we do have the option to refrain from saying something we shouldn't say or doing something we shouldn't do. We can make excuses and say this is who we are, this is how we feel, or this is how we think. But by not taking some ownership over the fact that we can actually control what we say and do, we are just being reckless.

Once again, I am brought back to the gentleman I worked with; for some reason, I can't get him off my mind while I am writing about this. It would have been pretty easy to tell him off or tell him to shape up. Honestly, it probably would have felt pretty good for a minute or two, just to tell him how awful he was treating people and how hard it was to be around him or talk to him. I could have told him how much I tried to avoid him at times because I couldn't handle his attitude. I have been tempted a few times to do that with various people over the years.

I am sure I have given into that feeling more than once, and I have no doubt people have wanted to say something to me about my attitude as well. It is hard not to go there sometimes, but we have the choice to be kind or not. Be patient or not.

It is amazing to me how approaching someone with one attitude or another impacts the relationship and the interaction. The same is true when it comes to work. If I go into it with a negative attitude, the chances of me having a good day are pretty slim. Things could turn around, but they wouldn't need to turn around so much if I would have just chosen to be positive to begin with.

And I'm not saying you have to show up for work grinning ear to ear and throwing lollipops into the air. If you did that, people might lock you up for being a little on the crazy side. All it really takes is choosing not to give in to the drama that is around you. Not participating in gossip. Choosing to be courteous and kind to those around you, even when you don't feel like it.

Just like I had a choice of how I reacted to the gentleman I worked with, he had a choice of how he reacted to me. When I said good morning to him, he had the choice of being polite or being grouchy. If he was having a rough day and I happened to ask him how his day was going, he had a choice in how he delivered the information to me. He could choose to tell me that the day wasn't going great in a harsh or mellow tone. How he approached others was his choice, not determined by his situation or current frustration. Well, it didn't have to be. We didn't have to become victims of his attitude; he chose that for us. And no one should be a victim of ours.

We all react incorrectly or deal with situations the wrong way from time to time. When it becomes a constant way of being, a continuous point of view and your first response 99 percent of the time, that is a problem. And it can keep you from a lot of great things that could happen.

Attitude is important to think about because it can change the trajectory of your life. It can change for better or worse. Which way it goes is up to you.

You can alienate yourself from everyone and choose to be a victim. You can choose to criticize everyone and everything and push the possibilities away from you. You can decide to live in isolation and misery. You can choose to focus on everything that is wrong with the world, your life, your family, your job and everyone you meet. You can choose that. It is an option that is yours for the taking.

You also have the choice to become victorious in your own life, in whatever way you define that. You can encourage those around you and see the possibilities and opportunities around you. You can see hard situations as chances to grow and become a better person. You can live in community, whether that means having a few reliable friends or a big group of people you spend time with. You can choose to see the positives in your world, your life, your family, your job and everyone you meet as you focus on fixing the areas that you feel need attention and change. You can choose that. This option is also yours for the taking.

Which sounds like a better life and existence to you?

Choosing your attitude takes work. It takes time to train yourself to be able to step outside the circumstances and see what your opportunities really are. Deciding to act and react better takes time to figure out, especially if you are used to focusing on everything that's awful about your life and your world. If you have been stuck in that headspace for a while, it will take time to get unstuck and train your brain to take a new approach to life. But it is worth the effort.

Bottom line: living in unnecessary misery is a waste of good energy.

I recently had some issues with my back that tested me on this whole idea of choosing your attitude. Other than when I broke my toe, I had never really been through an experience like it before. I was limited physically, and it was emotionally draining. I was trying to lose weight at the time (still am) and because my back was so out of whack, working out wasn't an option. In the past, every time I had tried to lose weight, I had to both eat well and workout.

Unfortunately for me, for about four months, working out wasn't an option, particularly in the beginning of the whole ordeal.

It was tough, not being able to do the simplest activities and needing people to help me with things I felt I should be able to do for myself. It was exhausting, but I knew that my best chance at getting through it was staying positive and focusing on getting better, not on what I wasn't able to do at that point.

During that four-month period, I focused on what I could do to get better and did everything I could to stay on the positive track. I had days where I gave in to the negativity. My friends could tell you some of my harder days were filled with a lot of whining, but I fought through it because I didn't want it to derail everything I had accomplished up to that point and didn't want it to hold me back either.

The experience tested my patience and my attitude, but it taught me once again that I had the control on whether or not the situation was going to hold me back. I had the choice of how I was going to treat my family, friends, and coworkers. I was in pain, and I was struggling, but I didn't have to take it out on the people who were trying to help me or the ones who were paying my salary.

I had a choice. It was hard sometimes, but I knew it was up to me to get through it without completely imploding my life and setting myself back. My attitude was my choice. During that time, I was able to regain perspective on how each little step forward I take counts for something and adds up to something great. Which was the most amazing lesson I could learn!

Attitude is important. It helps direct our course. It helps us gain or lose relationships. It helps us gain or lose opportunities in all areas of our lives. Sometimes it is easy to forget how powerful our attitude can be and how much it can influence the course of our lives but make no mistake, it does.

One of my favorite quotes about attitude comes from the book *Vision to Reality* by Honorée Corder, and I think it is a great way to close this chapter.

> *Remember, "be, do, and have." You must be positive and then do the right things to have (get) what you want. To be enthusiastic, you must decide to be enthusiastic.*
>
> *Think positive. Read positive. Listen positive. Talk positive. Affirm positive. Watch positive. Practice positive. Make yourself positive.*[8]

Your attitude can direct which way your day goes, and that is up to you. Do you want to spend today being miserable? Or do you want to focus on what is good, what is important, and continue to move forward?

The choice is up to you.

Chapter review:

Your attitude can propel you forward, or it can hold you back. Which one it does is really up to you.

We can be victims or we can be victors in our lives.

Your attitude can keep the people you might really need in your life from getting close to you.

Living in unnecessary misery is a waste of good energy.

Your attitude attracts or repels people in your life. It also attracts or repels opportunities.

Take action challenge!

Did you want another challenge? Here ya go!

Our attitudes are so powerful. How we approach people and talk to ourselves can change the direction and focus of our day. It is truly amazing. Are you struggling with your attitude? Are you feeling weighed down and burdened by it? Is there a relationship you have that is making it hard for you to be positive at home or work? I want to challenge you, right now, to think about that situation. What can you do to improve it? What choices can you make to improve the situation and begin to take control of your attitude?

Take action now!

Waiting for perfect is never as smart as making progress.

~ Seth Godin

CHAPTER 6

PROGRESS OVER PERFECTION

One of my major struggles in the pursuit of change is the longing for perfection. My desire is not for just the plan to be perfect, but for the process and journey to be perfect as well. I also tend to have this unrealistic expectation of myself to be perfect, no matter what happens. I build this master plan with all these stepping stones to help me get to the end goal. I think to myself how amazing the process is going to be. I have everything figured out; I know exactly what I need to do and how to get to the end.

This is going to be perfect. Things are going to line up like I dreamed they would. Everything is going to add up to the perfect picture in my mind. This is going to be the most incredible journey ever!

I am sure you can guess the end of this story here, the end of all of my stories that start out with these grand plans which include this mindset from the get-go. Eventually, reality hits and I feel like my perfect plan was destroyed.

And that it was destroyed by me, the one who can't do anything right or perfect. I end up feeling discouraged, distraught, frustrated, and a host of other emotions. And many times, my lack of perfection and the feeling of falling short of my irrational expectations leads me to a place of just giving up for a while. I put my plans on the back burner once again, letting valuable time pass because, essentially, I broke my own heart by not succeeding as I had hoped. I set myself up, fell for the lie of perfection and put myself back in a position I had been in multiple times before. Ugh.

Perfection is a fun idea. It is fun to dream in that headspace, being able to knock out milestone after milestone, check things off the list in perfect order, achieve goals exactly when you plan to. To be honest, it makes me happy just thinking about it. I love the fresh idea, the plan, and how beautiful it is in my mind. However, I can say that 100 percent of the time, it doesn't work out the way I thought or hoped it would. The idea can be fantastic, the plan can be impeccable, but it never goes exactly the way it is laid out.

We talked a little about how your plans need to be dynamic and flexible when you are making changes to your life. This touches along those same lines.

Sometimes even when we do everything we are supposed to do, we check every box and cross every "t," the expected result is somehow not achieved. This happens to me during the process of weight loss. It drives me crazy, but sometimes I do everything I should. I exercise like I should, eat pretty well, and do enough to lose a specific amount of weight... and the scale says, "Nope!" Sometimes the opposite happens too, where I don't do everything I should, and the results still show up. It's confusing and a little maddening, too. How can a person do everything they are supposed to do and end up in completely the wrong place? It happens.

What else happens? You can get off track in your pursuit of executing your perfect plan. Something occurs, and you find yourself failing to take some steps forward or check things off your list. Life blindsides you, or you take a day off as a reward, but instead that one day off turns into a week or a month. And then you think you can start over. A whole new plan! That's exactly what you need, right? It was the plan that failed you. Now it's time to invest in building an entirely new one, and that will allow you to achieve your goal in the most perfect way. This time you will follow through, this time you will see success, this time will be different.

Then history repeats itself, and the cycle continues. Things fall apart, you fail to do something necessary, life happens, or whatever else causes your perfect plan to fail you. And once again you think this new plan, this new way of doing things, is going to be the ticket to everything you've ever wanted.

And on and on it goes.

Believe me, I have been there before. I tend to live out this cycle from time to time. I used to do it all the time, thinking that it was the plan that was wrong. I thought the plan needed tweaking or a complete makeover and then I would be able to achieve the things I was attempting to do. That was how it worked, right? The perfect plan—the one just right for me—was out there, I just needed to find it. That was the answer to my problems.

Unfortunately, or fortunately, I was wrong. Very wrong.

The truth is, the plan could be impeccable, and it could look at your situation from all different angles. It could take into consideration all kinds of variables and ideas and possibilities, but it will still fall short. Not sure if that is harder for you to hear, or harder for me to type. There is a part of me that will always cling to the idea of the perfect plan. I don't know why perfection is something that we feel compelled to have. Maybe we want others to see what great things we are doing, to prove to them how amazing we are in some way. Maybe we want to prove to ourselves that we are amazing. I don't know why it matters so much to some of us, but it does. And that, my friends, is something we need to let go of.

I am not saying you shouldn't try to do things well, that you should put in less effort or not try to do your very best. The inability to do everything perfectly or carry out the perfect plan does not excuse a person from putting in an effort. You will not get that excuse from me! What I want you to understand, and what I want to grasp onto myself as well, is that the ambition of perfection is a trap that keeps you from moving forward, making an effort and implementing change. If all you are trying to do is be perfect, all the time, with everything you do, you are going to end up discouraged, disheartened and more likely to give up.

I don't want that to be where you end up. I don't want to end up there myself.

Having a great plan is a great place to start. It can contain everything you want to happen and make you dream in new ways. Attack it, live it. But don't get caught up in this idea of perfection. Do your best, do well, and give it everything you have until you have nothing left. Push yourself, demand great effort from yourself, but don't beat yourself up for not reaching the heights of success if you fall short a little. Because, frankly, it is going to happen.

You set a goal to lose this many pounds or save that amount of money in a particular time frame. You put your heart and soul into it and find yourself a few pounds or dollars short. When you come to this place, in reality, you have two options on how you approach this situation. I am sure a person could come up with more than two, but the following are the two that I prefer to focus on.

You can choose to label yourself a failure. You got to a decent point, but it's not where you intended to be. You can beat yourself for falling short and not being good enough, perfect enough or strong enough.

Or.

You can choose to label yourself as a success. You didn't hit the numbers you were hoping for, which is disappointing, but you made progress. You are closer to your goal than you were before. How can that not be a win? Yes, you didn't achieve what you set out to, but you are not just closer to the end goal you started with, but now you also have experience from your effort that will help you shape the next phase of your journey.

It is all about seeing your progress instead of focusing on what you failed to achieve. Making progress, pushing forward, learning lessons, doing better—that is the meat and potatoes of making life changes. Real life changes.

If you want to remain stuck and label yourself with all kinds of negative words, focusing on your lack of ability to achieve perfection, you will continue living in a vicious cycle and get nowhere near where you say you want to be.

On the other hand, if you focus on the progress you have made, identify the lessons you have learned from your experience, and continue to make an effort in moving forward, you are going to get closer to your goals in a shorter amount of time. I can guarantee that.

When I looked up the word "perfect" in the dictionary, a couple of words popped out at me. "Absolute" and "complete."[9] I don't know how you would interpret that, but to me, those word associations are very telling when it comes to our pursuit of goals and attaching this idea of perfection to them.

When things are absolute or complete, they are done. There are no lessons to be learned. They are over. They are in the past. There are no more steps to take, and things are finished. When we think of changing our lives and reaching our goals, the journey never really ends. Yes, you might hit a goal and be done with that one, but what usually happens? You set another one, and then another one. You achieve a specific goal and set a similar one a level higher. A few more pounds lost, a few more dollars saved.

It may seem like a goal has been completed, and in a sense it has, but in the big picture of our lives, it's part of a whole journey. It is a stepping stone to get to the next thing and the next. In the pursuit of perfection, we can miss this idea that life doesn't work that way. Even though we can check something off our list, we are never completely done with it because there is a whole new level to chase after and achieve.

I just love the way that sounds. I love this idea that I'm a work in progress, that my life is something I have to continually work on. I think I would get bored if I didn't feel like there was more to pursue and change. Sometimes it'd be good if things were all figured out, if things were complete and I didn't have to put any more effort into them. Not going to lie, that thought is sometimes appealing.

However, the whole process of change is my lifeblood. If I am not changing, working toward something, or setting goals in multiple areas of my life, I am not really living. If I ever get to that point, I honestly don't think I could continue on. The process of growth is what keeps me alive, and I hope that you have some of that in your own life.

I hope that you aren't seeking perfection so much that you are losing out on the beauty of progress. Because, honestly, it is quite breathtaking. Sometimes it is a mess, but it is one beautiful mess.

Perfection is a trap that we can all get stuck in from time to time. It is that monster in your closet telling you that each goal has to be completed by a certain date and if it isn't, you've failed. That you have to cross off every single thing on your to-do list for the day and if you haven't, you've failed. That you are required to lose ten pounds in the next month and if you only lose nine, you've failed. Perfection is an evil little bugger that steals the joy you could and should have because of the things you have accomplished.

The pursuit of perfection will tell you all kinds of lies, and if you believe them, you will live your life discouraged and disheartened. I don't want that life for you. I don't want you to spend all your time on this planet feeling like you've failed or that you aren't good enough. I don't want that for you, and I hope you want more for yourself than that.

When we begin to focus our energy on progress instead of perfection in our pursuit of changing our lives, we can make so much more headway. That is just a fact. Rather than getting hung up on where we fall short, we see the value in what we are doing and achieving. The most amazing thing about focusing on our progress over this idea of perfection is that it allows us to see lessons we may not have seen before.

When we are concentrating on our progress and our process, we are more apt and open to different ideas. We are also able to see different possibilities that come our way, which in turn can get us closer to another milestone in our journey. If we focus on being perfect, instead of seeing the life lessons that are in front of us during our journey, we are wasting energy looking at what we didn't do, what we feel we failed at. And by doing that, we could be missing out on a lesson that could boost our efforts.

I want you to take a moment and think about your own journey. Not the one you are about to take as you read this book, but your life up to this point. How many times have you beaten yourself up mentally for not achieving a goal, not following through, not being perfect? How many times have you compared your life to someone else's and thought you had failed by comparison?

As I have been writing, I have been thinking about these questions for myself. How many times have I beaten myself up for not achieving a goal, for not being better, smarter, or further along in life? How many times have I convinced myself that I am failing adulthood because my life doesn't look a certain way, mostly compared to the lives of other people my age? As I was asking myself these questions, I shifted my focus from my lack of perfection and the failures I can point out in my life and looked at my life from the perspective of progress.

I am not the same person I was fifteen years ago. I guess most of us are not, but for me, I feel like the differences are drastic in some ways. I am a lot more confident, I know who I am, I know what my triggers are, I know how to deal with a lot of relationships I have, I don't waste a lot of time apologizing for the things I need. I'm far from perfect, but that isn't something any of us can achieve. I have made progress, though. I have changed a lot.

Because I have focused so much of my energy to change in my adult life, I have changed. If I wouldn't have made the conscious decision to keep improving myself and my life, I don't know where I would be right now. Or if I would even be here anymore. Are things amazing all the time? Far from it. I struggle with various things like anyone else, but because I have chosen to focus my energy on learning what I can do in order to move forward in life, life is pretty sweet even when things aren't going my way.

I don't have it all figured out, but I know I never will. And that is okay. I will keep learning, keep pushing forward, keep absorbing the lessons I need to learn from my past and present and apply them as I move forward. That is the best way to live, at least from my own experience.

Comparing ourselves to others is something that can cause us to see ourselves in less-than-favorable ways. Not only that, but it perpetuates this idea of perfection. Comparison is a trap when it comes to how we deal with change. It is so easy to get caught up in what everyone else is doing and where everyone is going. This person has so much money, or that person is working their dream career. This person has the family life I've always wanted, or that person gets to travel the world like I have always dreamed of doing. Whatever it is, we compare our lives to the lives of those around us. And with social media, it is even harder to avoid the insanity of comparison. We have access to so many people and see these seemingly perfect lives displayed in front of us. We forget that behind those perfect pictures are individuals who have struggles and insecurities like the rest of us do.

It is easy to let these things get to us and distract us from what is true and important. It is easy to let these things eat us alive inside and keep us from stepping forward in our own lives. Sometimes it can feel like we are punishing ourselves for not being further in our lives or not achieving what others have. This is unfair to ourselves and not to mention a waste of valuable energy.

Don't waste time comparing yourself to others. I know it isn't that simple or that easy to avoid all the time, but don't dwell on what others are doing. If they are doing something you want to do, use it as inspiration to change your own life; learn from what they are doing and maybe even reach out to them to see if they have any helpful advice. Don't live in jealousy and wish for something someone else has, especially if you are unwilling to take the steps forward to get somewhere better yourself.

Change is difficult to do sometimes. It is hard to give up on this idea of perfection. It is hard to believe that it can't be an option sometimes. I wish it were possible more often, but aiming for perfection can only get you so far. And it can lead to a place of discontent, self-hatred, self-loathing and a whole mess of emotions that I don't want you to waste your time having if you can help it.

Will you have days when you falter and focus on the things that bring you down from time to time? Yes. You're human. Will you wish for an easier route? Yes. Will you want to achieve perfect results? Can we all say it together here? YES. You will have these days. I will have these days. They are unavoidable.

But remember, we can choose to adjust our thinking and focus on the things that not only matter but actually get us to where we want to be. We can choose to focus on the process of progress instead of drowning in the idea and myth of perfection. We all have that choice, whether we choose to believe it or not.

Choosing to focus on our effort and our progress is what is going to save us a lot of time and a lot of heartache as well. It is going to get us where we want to go. Focusing on what we have control over and taking ownership of those things is vital in our pursuit of becoming better people and changing our lives. Focusing on our progress instead of dwelling on where we fell short is going to save us from hurt that we don't need to feel for extended periods of time. Disappointment will happen, and that hurts, and it is fine to feel that feeling. In fact, it is healthy to acknowledge those kinds of emotions. However, setting up camp there and remaining there for long periods of time is not healthy and not what I want for you.

If you fall short of the idea, the dream, or the goal you've set for yourself, feel the emotions that come along with that but don't remain there. Look at what you can learn from the experience that you just had, celebrate the progress you have made, and move forward.

Let go of the idea of things being perfect and life happening exactly the way you planned it out to be.

Remember, plans and life are dynamic. They change with the wind. Don't get caught up in a perfect picture or process and lose out on the opportunity and chance to move forward, better and wiser than before.

Choose to focus on progress over perfection.

Chapter review:

If all you are trying to do is be perfect, all the time, with everything you do, you are going to end up discouraged, disheartened and more likely to give up.

Making progress, pushing forward, learning lessons, and doing better is how you make real life changes.

Perfection steals the joy you could and should have because of the things you have accomplished.

You can choose to focus on the process of progress instead of drowning in the idea and myth of perfection.

Focusing on the things you have control over and taking ownership of them is vital in your pursuit of becoming a better person and changing your life.

Take action challenge!

Are you ready for a challenge? Let's do this!

The process of change is a tough one and chasing the idea of perfection makes it that much harder! It is time to let that go, don't you think? I have a challenge for you. What if you were to sit down tonight and make a list of all the things you did today in order to move toward a better life? What would that list include? Take out a piece of paper and write down what you have accomplished in the past twenty-four hours that has improved your situation. If you want to take it a step further, commit to doing this for the next seven days.

Not only will it feel good to see what you have accomplished, but it will also give you insight into which tasks are more important and which are getting you closer to the life you want to create for yourself.

Take action now!

Surround yourself with positive people.

~ Melanie Fiona

CHAPTER 7

FIND YOUR PEOPLE

When you begin the process of changing your life, it is possible you could experience pushback from the people around you. It is a strange phenomenon, but sometimes the people from whom you expect the most support are the ones who have the most negative things to say. I know I have experienced this before, and I am guessing you have as well. I have heard so many people talk about this, from authors to podcasters, so I know it isn't an uncommon thing, but even though I know it is true, it always takes me by surprise. You expect that the ones who love you are going to be excited for the journey you are about to take. You expect them to be your cheerleaders and wish you the best of luck or offer support right from the get-go.

However, it doesn't always work that way. For whatever reason, those who are closest to you or who have known you for a long time question your ideas, your plans, and your goal of achieving something new and different. There are a few different reasons for that, which I feel are important to cover as we continue our discussion about the process of change.

Oftentimes, the people who are putting down our dreams and plans and making negative comments about the goals we have are not doing so from a bad place. They could truly believe we are capable of doing whatever it is we are setting out to do, and they may even want it for us on some level, but their reaction and words come off telling us a different story. This is common, though it doesn't make it sting any less. I want you to take heart knowing that this isn't an unusual thing and that there are ways to deal with this, which I will cover a little later. For right now, know you aren't alone here.

Have you ever told someone about a goal of yours that was entirely realistic and doable, and they came back with some warning or some comment that suggested they thought it was a bad idea? Or that it is too risky or just not you? You came to them full of excitement about this idea that you have put a great deal of thought into and in a split second, they have decided for whatever reason that it might be too much for you. That this endeavor is outside your abilities, your capabilities or maybe even your personality. Or maybe you have something in your past that suggests to them that you can't or shouldn't do this particular thing, and they are making an effort to remind you of that.

I think it is important for me to take a step back here and say something because it is the truth. Sometimes they are right. Sometimes the other person has reason to question something you want to do. Sometimes they may have legitimate concerns you need to consider. So I don't want you to automatically disregard everything others might have to say every single time. They may have a point of view that could help you think the situation through better or help you see it from a different angle. Be open to this possibility because, in the end, it could save you from a great deal of heartache and struggle.

However, they aren't always right to question your ideas, plans, and goals. Their comments, negativity, and warnings are not always justified. You must learn to recognize when it is a good idea to listen to them and when to let it roll off your back.

Sometimes the things people say are said out of their own fears. It comes from a place within them that says they could never do this, they could never achieve this, they could never try to accomplish something so big. People project their fears onto others. We all do it. I try to be aware that my journey is different, my natural abilities are different, and, of course, my goals are not the same as the person next to me, so someone else's plan for change would or could terrify me if I were to go down that path. The people in your life may want to protect you from getting hurt or taking risks, but many times their reaction comes from a place of their own deep-rooted fears. They look at this beautiful idea and plan you have and think from their own perspective instead of yours.

Why? Because they can't see it from your viewpoint. If they truly are close to you and understand you, then there is a possibility of them being able to connect with your plan.

When I made the decision to move to Portland in 2014, I knew that it wouldn't be a popular decision with some. I knew people would worry about me, even though I wasn't apprehensive at all. Honestly, I wasn't fearful. I was going to a new city and moving into a neighborhood I had never been in before, but I was confident in my ability to make it work. I knew I could do it, and I knew how important it was to me. It was a longtime dream of mine, and I knew this was my chance to make it happen.

Before I told many people about what I was going to do, I made sure I was confident in the idea. I knew that if I went to those close to me with this plan before thinking it through and sorting through all my own doubts about it, I would be at risk for being talked out of it. Not intentionally; I don't want to make it sound like people in my life wouldn't have been supportive. But I do think if I hadn't been 100 percent convinced of the idea myself before going to them, any negative comment, or any comment that I interpreted as negative for that matter, would have derailed the whole plan. I needed to be in a stable place myself with the whole idea before inviting anyone else into it. If I was going to choose not to move forward with it, I wanted it to be because I had made that choice and not because I didn't get the support I had hoped for or because someone had said something negative.

Sometimes people can only see life through their own filter. They can only understand life from their point of view and cannot step into your shoes to look at life the way you do. Knowing this reality is something you need to embrace as you go through this journey of change so you don't allow others to derail you from achieving something because of their reactions, whether that was their intention or not.

Don't let their words become your words, or their feelings become yours. Don't completely disregard what others have to say, but don't let others influence you away from changing your life for the better and achieving goals that are achievable. Don't let others have that much power over you.

Some people didn't understand my decision to move to Portland. It was a goal of mine since age sixteen, but I hadn't made it known. So when it came time for me to go, and I finally shared it with people, the shock was understandable. To me, it was something that had always been a part of my life and that I had wanted for a long time. For others, it was brand-new information.

Understand that you need to give some grace to those in your life when they react to your plan. If this is brand-new information, you may need to give them time to process it. Their responses may come off worse than they may mean to because they feel a little blindsided. Give them a break, allow them to absorb the information and do not take their initial response too personally, especially if these people are your closest family and friends. They might be surprised to find out they didn't know you as well as they thought.

Everyone sees the world differently, which shouldn't be a surprise to you. What is important to you isn't necessarily important to other people. What you choose to pursue, some would find crazy. And because we have these differences between us, we need to be able to understand that reactions are going to vary from person to person and situation to situation.

Once again, I feel the need to say that not everything people say in response to your plans is going to be wrong or without some merit. I will readily admit that I have rolled my eyes plenty of times at some of the things my parents have said to me, as a caution, warning or concern. They haven't always been wrong. (You're welcome, Mom and Dad!) Much of the advice they gave me was something I should have considered at the very least.

It is hard when the people around you don't understand what you are doing or why you are doing it. It is hard when the people around you are toxic and negative. Don't let this discourage you from doing what you need to do to move forward. I know it is easy for me to say that since I don't live in your shoes. I don't know your situation or see the relationship dynamics that play out in your daily life. And I am not going to pretend to know how you live or how things affect you.

Some people won't understand your journey. Some will applaud your efforts. Some may look at you sideways. Despite the reactions you may receive, you must push forward and continue on your journey to change your life.

When it comes to going after goals that change your life, you have to find some inner peace and understanding with your plans. You have to realize that people will have their reactions and comments. You can listen to them, then choose to let them go or take them to heart. You can be confident in your plan or readjust your plan if need be. You also have to realize that your path isn't meant to be a mirror image of someone else's. It shouldn't be; I mean, how boring would that be? That doesn't mean it can't be similar, but you aren't supposed to live the exact same life as everyone around you. God made us as individuals, and we should live as such. He didn't mean for us to squelch our dreams and put the desires He has placed on our hearts into a box. We were not designed to be someone we are not.

When you have a passion for something that the people in your life don't seem to understand, it is crucial to seek out others who do. People who are on similar journeys or have a similar mindset. Though the people around you love you, they may not be able to put themselves in a place to truly understand how deep the passion goes inside of you. Don't have that expectation of them and do be understanding when they seem confused. And in the meantime, find people who can join the journey. In this day and age, it is easier than ever to find a community of people who can become your tribe.

I have found a few groups like this, and just knowing that there are other people out there seeking change and chasing similar goals or interests to mine, trying to grow and learn and become better people, keeps me going. It keeps me focused. I do have a few great friends that support my goals and have been so encouraging while I have pursued different goals. I have a few friends that check in with me on how my writing is going and how much I've accomplished, which has been such a blessing. Though some of them don't write themselves, they understand how important it is to me and support my goal to publish a book and in return do what they can to encourage me.

Seek out a community. Find like-minded people in your area. And if there isn't a community for your particular interests and goals, be brave and create one! Another option would be to move. Sometimes you have to get bold, step way outside your box, and go where you need to go. Just like a musician moving to Nashville to be closer to the heart of music and other artists, sometimes that step is necessary. It is important to take steps to find others who share your passion. It is something that will help keep it alive in you.

Finding people who can truly be your tribe and encourage you as you pursue change is a big deal. If you are surrounded by people who don't get your dream or don't quite get you at all, it can feel lonely and in turn discourage you from going after something that is truly important to you. And once again, they may not mean to discourage you from anything, but it can come off that way.

People are not always going to understand the passion you have for something, and that is okay. You are meant to pursue the things you love and which keep you going. You are meant to live a full life and not one that is filled with someone else's goals and dreams. You can help others with theirs, and that can be part of your dream, but you need to have some ownership in it.

When it comes to the reaction of others, you have to be ready for the whole spectrum that is out there. You never know who is going to react which way, and you might be surprised by what comes out of some people's mouths. Those you expect to mock you could be supportive. Those you expect to fully support you may feel blindsided and, ultimately, try to talk you out of it.

This is a huge part of changing your life, especially if you are doing it in a big and noticeable way. The more you grow, the more people notice, the more people question you, the stronger your convictions need to be to stick to your plan, stick to your goal, improve your life and become the best you possible. The more you need community.

There may be times when setting up boundaries in particular relationships becomes necessary; when that is appropriate is something you will need to decide for yourself. There are times when a connection with someone is so toxic that setting a boundary is the best option you have, other than cutting them out of your life completely. Sometimes when you take this kind of action, you can actually bring balance to the relationship and allow each side a great deal of peace.

Is there a topic of conversation that comes up that each of you get riled up about? Maybe a boundary you could set up is steering clear of that specific topic or changing the subject when it is brought up. Do you spend a lot of time with someone who is toxic or negative or just puts you in a bad place mentally in some way? Maybe a boundary you can put in place is a time limit on the connection. Instead of opting to cut them out of your life completely, you could choose to connect with them once a week.

This is not always the easiest thing to follow through on. You may feel like a mean person, a selfish person. And I don't want to encourage you to live a selfish life, but you have to realize that taking care of yourself is important too. Who you surround yourself with and who you are connected to impacts your day-to-day life and that trickles into your life as a whole

Not every journey of change requires a complete 180 turnaround in one's life, however, it does require devotion, and often radical devotion.

You need to commit to this journey of change. You need to embrace the passion you have for this new path, this new way of living. You have to decide that you are no longer going to settle for what is in front of you and commit to creating a better life for yourself and those you care for. You have to commit to giving up a mediocre life and stop settling for whatever crosses your path.

CHOOSE CHANGE

You have to choose this journey with your whole being. Maybe your motivation is to help others, or to impact the life of your family in some way; both are great things, but ultimately, this journey has to begin within yourself. And once you have done that, it is time to seek out your community.

Chapter review:

Don't disregard everything others might have to say about your plans for change. They may have a point of view that could help you think the situation through better or help you see it from a different angle.

Sometimes people project their worries onto you due to their own deep-rooted fears.

Your path isn't meant to be a mirror image of someone else's.

When you have a passion for something that the people in your life don't seem to understand, it is important to seek out people who do.

The more you grow, the more people notice, the more people question you, and the stronger your convictions need to be to stick to your plan, stick to your goal, improve your life and become the best you possible.

Take action challenge!

Challenge time!

It is important for everyone to have people they can count on in all seasons of life, whether or not they are on a journey to change their life. And that includes YOU! Do you have a group of people you can count on? Do you have the support you need to move forward with your goals? This is something I want to encourage you to pursue with some intention. So often, our goals fall by the wayside because we do not surround ourselves with like-minded people and end up losing our momentum. It is time for you to expand your circle!

Take a minute to think about what your goals are and then think of ways to actively seek out people who are after the same or similar goals. Is there a group you can join? Or create? Are there people at your church or place of employment you can connect with? There are people out there! Seek out support!

Take action now!

Continuous effort – not strength or intelligence – is the key to unlocking our potential.

~ Winston Churchill

CHAPTER 8

FOLLOW THROUGH

I am not sure what comes to your mind when you think of willpower, but for me, it is this magical and mythical thing that lives out in the forest somewhere. Willpower is something we all want, but it seems like we can't hold onto it for very long, doesn't it? What does it even mean to have it? And how do we lose it?

You tell someone that you are struggling to stay on track with the change you are trying to make and the common response is, "You just need more willpower."

My internal response is usually, "What does that even mean? Is there some place I can buy some?"

Instead of focusing on willpower, I prefer to concentrate on following through. The act of following through on what you said you would do. Choosing the actions and then completing them to get to the desired result.

Follow-through is what gets a person from point A to point B, and beyond. Taking the action necessary in order to achieve your goals is what is required for making changes in your life. Big or small. The act of following through is what gets you where you want to go.

In short, change takes effort. And most importantly, it is required even when you have no desire to do it or your focus is elsewhere.

Effort is how you get from where you are to where you want to be. Period. End of story.

Effort is hard work; effort is time. It is what makes you a millionaire, makes you healthy, and makes you smarter and whatever else it is you desire to be. Putting in effort is what makes athletes as good as they are, what makes writers sell more books, and what makes musicians wail on those guitars so effortlessly. Effort is what turns the mailroom boy into a CEO, the student into the professor, the poor man into a rich one. Without the effort and follow-through, these individuals would not have been able to get to where they are. There are those who are true geniuses, who come out of the womb able to do amazing things or who are born into money, allowing them to reach great heights much faster. However, many of the people we admire who have extreme talent or wealth did not come from these places, although they look like they might have.

They are self-made. And they got there with effort and with follow-through.

When we rely on willpower to get us to where we want to be, we forget one key truth about life and human nature: feelings are fickle. They seem to change with the wind. We can be excited about something one minute and loathing it the next. I have to laugh at myself because I am feeling that way right now. Yesterday, I was so excited about a plan I set up for myself for the next month. It's a great one, completely doable, and will be worth it in the end. I was on a high about it, probably partly due to the excitement of planning. (Seriously, I love it.) It is a great plan, though, and will certainly boost my results. It is just a matter of sticking with it. And let me tell you, today, I have no desire to. That little voice in my head is saying I can put it off and start Monday, but I know that will lead to more days off and more lost time.

My point is, feelings can change from minute to minute. And they can change because of a specific reason or just because we are human and that's what happens. Your ability to resist temptations or follow through on things regardless of how you are feeling gets easier as time goes on, as you make more and more efforts forward and follow through on your plans and goals.

Feelings about people, about situations, about food, about money, about your job and about your responsibilities all change throughout the day. You could care about weight loss at the beginning of the day, then lunchtime comes around and you think, "What is the harm in hitting up the fast food drive-thru?" Feelings are fickle. You might want to save for retirement or a big purchase you have been dreaming about, but you find yourself spending the evening online shopping and giving into an impulse buy because, well, you want it.

Feelings are fickle.

Feelings are not constant, and we have to stop pretending that they are. And we also have to stop using our feelings as an excuse to not follow through on responsibilities or the steps it takes to reach a goal.

When we start using our feelings as a reason to give up, take time off, or walk away from someone or something important, we are ultimately giving up our power to make positive and meaningful changes in our lives. We are also choosing to unfairly let ourselves down, not to mention the other people in our life. When we choose to do what feels good in the moment and let go of what matters to us, we can ultimately lose everything. If you choose the drive-thru more often than you should, choose to spend money instead of saving, or choose yourself over your relationships, you could end up unhealthy, broke, and alone. If you blindly follow your feelings, where is that going to get you?

I don't mean to sound overdramatic, but in reality, this is how things can play out. I previously mentioned that I have been dealing with some back issues for a while and during this whole ordeal, I have been reminding myself that the healing is happening, but it is happening bit by bit. Over time, little by little, we can get better, or we can get worse. We can improve, or we can deteriorate.

And that happens by the effort we take, despite our feelings. Not because of them, but in spite of them.

As much as I enjoy giving into the little things that keep me from my goals, in the end, I almost always end up feeling guilty, frustrated, and ticked off at myself for not following through on what I know is most important to me. Doing what feels good in the moment, more specifically when it is contrary to my goals, is almost always completely unsatisfying in the end. Giving in to my food cravings, spending money I shouldn't or don't have to spend, and sleeping in instead of getting up early to tackle my goals all sound great and even feel great momentarily. But the feeling wears off, and I am left regretting my decision, wishing I would have done what I had planned to do and completed the things that are more important to me.

Things that make you feel good in the moment—like that extra piece of pizza or that impulse buy at your favorite store—feel good at the time, but that feeling wears off. If you honestly want to change your life, it is important to remember that those fleeting moments of pleasure won't get you where you want to go.

What brings satisfaction that lasts, as well as boosting your ability to make better choices in the future, is follow-through. You might be sick of reading these words, but it's the truth. Especially if you have a compulsion that is hard to control or some kind addiction, those momentary lapses can lead to a derailment of your goals. The last thing I want for you is to lose momentum, lose time, and end up going in a direction you never intended to go. Chasing what gets you closer to your goals is what brings true fulfillment.

Are you going to be faulted for having an extra piece of pizza once in a while? Of course not. Are you going to go bankrupt for spending an extra fifty dollars at your favorite store? Probably not. I am not going to tell you that you can't indulge from time to time. I would never say that you can't go off plan a little. Those rare indulgences are fantastic and something a person should do here and there. Treats and rewards are a great thing.

The problem comes when you start allowing yourself to indulge regularly, not putting boundaries on those areas of struggle in your life. Allowing them to derail you from the big picture plan is when it becomes an issue. That is when you are in the danger zone and risk losing momentum toward the end goal.

One activity that has helped me the most with writing this book is getting up in the morning before work to write, which wasn't very easy for me, especially at first. I wouldn't consider myself a morning person. I wouldn't really consider myself a night owl anymore either, though, but I used to be. However, I have realized that getting certain things done before work changes the outlook of the day for me. I carry myself differently, I approach people differently, and I am much more productive.

Since I have never really been a morning person, getting up before six o'clock in the morning was not easy for me, but I did it. I won't tell you I did it every single day, because that would be a bold-face lie, and I don't want to do that. However, I will tell you that the mornings I did it, it was because I knew my day would be better because of it and because I want to be consistently following through on the things I have set out to do with my life. I wanted to make sure that I put in the effort to make my life different, to make my life better than it was yesterday.

I really didn't want to get up early most days especially in the beginning, but I did it because I knew it was my ticket to getting ahead and starting my day in a more positive way.

Remember, feelings are fickle. Even after months of getting up earlier on a regular basis, I still don't always feel like getting up. I don't always feel like writing or working out in the morning. I like my cozy bed, thank you very much. However, I have accepted the fact that spending extra time in my bed is not going to make things happen, change my life, make me a better person, or help others.

Sometimes I wish it did, but unfortunately, it doesn't. So, that means I must get up, face the day, and do what needs to be done. It may not always be exactly as planned, but I know that whether I do everything I planned for the morning or only a portion of it, my life will be better off because of it.

When you look up the word "effort," a few related words are endeavor, energy, work, and labor. That's exactly where our focus should be as we try to change our lives. The focus should be on the work it takes to get to the next level. Our focus should be on putting energy into the things that matter, regardless of our feelings and what mood we happen to be in at the time. I am not going to tell you to ignore the big stuff in your life or the things that desperately need your attention when life throws you a curveball. What I am going to tell you is that on a regular Tuesday when you feel like sleeping in, deciding against a healthy lunch, or doing some impulse buying online before bed, I want you to think about where your focus should be. I want you to think about where it is and what it should be on.

Are you choosing this activity, this thing, because of your mood or your feelings? It is important to analyze our actions and determine whether they are moving us forward or holding us back.

I will tell you right now, doing what it takes to accomplish a goal or change your life takes energy, and you aren't always going to be energetic about it. There will be moments, hours, and days where it isn't something you want to be doing.

When it comes to putting in effort and following through on the things that are important to you, it is going to take time to make that a habit. It takes time to build up muscle, to lose fat, to save money, to write a book, or to start a new career. Time is your ally here, but you need to utilize it for it to work for you. If you are going to truly change your life, it is going to take time for your new activities and habits, your new routine, to become natural to you. It is going to take time for you to feel compelled to do the things you need to do, so there might be some pushing on your part to make the new things happen in the beginning.

I am sure you have heard someone say that it takes 21 days for a new habit to form. Well, the question is, can that really be true?

Recently, I was listening to a podcast, *Achieve Your Goals with Hal Elrod*[10], where Jay Papasan was being interviewed, and the subject of habit came up. According to the research he had done, it took an average of 66 days for people to form a new habit. The earliest that people were able to form a habit was in 18 days, and the longest was 254 days. He stated that the danger of relying on any number at all, whether it is 21 days, 30 days, 90 days or what have you, is that people tend to "take their foot off the gas too early" and assume that that number is going to work for them. Then he said my favorite sentence of all in the podcast:

"If you really want to form a new habit, you have to stick with it until it's a habit."

That is a truth bomb right there. There is no magic number that is one size fits all. You don't do something for a certain amount of days and hope for the best. It could take you three weeks to create a new habit, or it could take you nine months. Not everyone is going to pick up a habit or change their routines in the same way or the same amount of time. You do the work; you put in the effort until a new lifestyle is created.

And I think we can take that a step further and say that not every habit you try to adopt into your life is going to take form in the same amount of time as another one. For example, you may want to form a habit around exercise and eating healthy. One of those might be easier to adopt into your life than the other. You may form a habit of exercising regularly within a few weeks, but the healthy eating side of things takes longer, or vice versa.

The point is, have a good attitude as you begin to change your routine, your habits. Go into this change excited about what amazing things will happen, because they will if you put in the effort. Also, go into this process understanding that there will be struggles and some adjustments you may need to make. The habits you want to create and the changes you are hoping to make might take some time to form; don't be discouraged by this. It is a common part of the process, so don't feel blindsided by it.

Work at it until it sticks, and then keep going.

What is really going to help you as you go through this process of changing your life is making both a mental and written commitment ahead of time. Writing down your goals and your plans only amplifies your chances of following through and accomplishing what it is you are setting out to do. Making a commitment beforehand and continually doing that as you go from day to day just compounds the intensity and dedication you have for what you are aiming for. Every night, I make a verbal commitment, with myself, to making my mornings count. I tell myself, out loud, that I am going to get up early, I am going to work out, and I am going to write. I don't tell myself I will try to, or that I hope to. I commit to doing it, without any hesitation. So when I wake up in the morning, the first thing on my mind is that commitment I made the night before. This is what I said I was going to do; I am going to do it.

Adjusting your life is important when you are attempting to change your life for the better. You can't do what you have always done and expect things to change. That just isn't how life works. If you want to accomplish a huge goal but don't want to put in the effort and energy to make adjustments to your life, chances are you won't be able to accomplish what it is you say you want to. It is really that simple. Life changes when you sacrifice, when you adjust, and when you choose to do more of the activities that get you closer to the end goal and less of the things that keep you where you are currently at.

Life changes when you choose to follow through and do the things that truly matter, that truly count. Simple, and as hard, as that.

Chapter review:

Following through and taking the action necessary in order to achieve your goals are required for making changes in your life. Big or small.

Feelings about people, about situations, about food, about money, about your job, or about your responsibilities all change throughout the day. Feelings are fickle.

Over time, little by little, you can get better, or you can get worse. You can improve, or you can deteriorate.

Giving in to impulses may feel good at the time, but they ultimately take you off track and can leave you feeling discouraged and upset with yourself.

When creating a habit, don't rely on a magic number. Work at it until it sticks.

Take action challenge!

Challenge? Yes, please!

Change takes effort. Simple as that. And sometimes, not so simple. It is much easier to say than do, isn't it? Like most things in life, it takes time and continual follow-through.
So, let's practice it! Like any change we want to make, there is an end goal in mind. To become the best or better at something or to create a new habit. What I am going to challenge you to do right now is to choose that thing you want to become more consistent at following through on. Could be working on a skill, reading a few pages of a book, writing a few words, exercising, encouraging friends, cooking healthy meals, or a number of another things.

I want you to commit right now to taking the first step forward and decide you are going to do this activity for seven days. It may not become a habit in that time frame, but if you look back and realize what you were able to accomplish and feel the great feelings that come along with that, I know you'll feel amazing and want to continue.

Take action now!

Success is a series of small wins.

~ Jaime Tardy

CHAPTER 9

CELEBRATE EFFORT

You are going to need something to keep you going when you begin changing your life, especially when your life situation changes. It is important to have something that helps you stay on track and not give up this new life you are trying to build for both yourself and those in your life. This is where rewards come in. Who doesn't love a good reward?

I think it is important to choose milestones in your journey to celebrate. These would be big things like hitting the halfway mark of your weight loss goal or hitting a new level with your fitness. You aim for a milestone to hit the big end goal you have planned.

Sometimes it is a good idea to set smaller milestone goals in addition to the larger ones to make an even bigger impact on your journey toward change. I call these benchmarks. I love celebrating the smaller increments that got me to the bigger goal. Benchmarks help you track your success and keep you motivated; when you hit a certain number of books read, pounds lost, money saved, or whatever it is you are trying to accomplish. If you are attempting to create new habits and reach thirty or sixty days of following through on that particular activity, that is something that could and should be celebrated. Having something to aim for and knowing when you have reached a new level is something that will propel you forward and keep you moving toward your end goal. It will help you to continue to make positive changes in your life and make you more excited to do what needs to be done to get to the next benchmark so that you can hit the milestone.

Celebrating both the big and small achievements that are going to ultimately help you get to the life you have been working toward should be a priority in your journey. As I said before, it can help propel you further and give you the spark you need to get through the challenging times that come your way. Each celebration doesn't need to be a grand party. You don't need to buy yourself a present for each accomplishment, especially if you are trying to change several different things. I have to admit, it would be fun to be able to do that, but it would be frivolous as well. Not only that, but it would also take away from the achievement and cheapen it. Achieving a goal, hitting a new milestone or even a small benchmark should be satisfactory enough on its own.

Being able to acknowledge what we have done is hard sometimes. A person can get caught up in life and stuck in their own head as well and not be able to see the amazing things they have done or how far they have actually come. The ability to step outside yourself and see the real picture is going to make a difference. It will help you find things to celebrate even when you feel like you aren't doing enough.

When I am feeling like I am not making any progress, or have nothing to be proud of, I ask myself some questions to try to figure out what the truth is. That way, I can get out of the vicious cycle that would more than likely start building in my head before it has a chance to take root.

I ask myself, where am I now in comparison to a month ago? What progress have I made? What have I learned? Am I the same person? Have I put in an effort? Have I gained perspective? Asking yourself great questions can open your mind to the truth and see what it is you are actually accomplishing, even if it feels like you are only treading water.

While asking yourself these questions, you can also begin to see any issues you may not have noticed before. Maybe you were doing something you thought was helping you change your life, but in the end, it is only keeping you from accomplishing vital steps or is wasting time. Maybe you see things from a perspective that is incorrect. Maybe you are leaning on the wrong people or following a plan that isn't quite up to the task or doesn't fit your life anymore. And while you are taking stock of what is happening and what you are doing, you are going to see not just where you might be falling short, but also the areas in your life in which you are succeeding as well. You will see where you are results, and that will allow you to recognize what you should be celebrating and patting yourself on the back for.

If you are making an effort, if you are trying, if you are doing what you can to take steps forward, I can guarantee you that there is something to be proud of yourself for, something to celebrate. Guaranteed.

When it comes to celebrations, I want you to consider celebrating the effort as well. Your effort. Sometimes the results take time to really show up in our lives, and it can be disheartening to wait for the fruits of your labor to be more visible. You are putting in the work, the hours, the time, the energy. You are sacrificing sleep and giving up some of your free time that you could be spending with friends or on your hobbies, and the results are just not coming the way you thought they would.

I believe they are coming. They will come. Maybe a small adjustment to what you are doing might be in order, who knows, but if you are putting in an effort, something will come of it. And you might be surprised to find out what it is. You just have to keep pushing and celebrate your effort.

One thing I have found very helpful in acknowledging and celebrating the small things is making a list at the end of the night of what I accomplished that day. It doesn't have to be super detailed or very long, but it is a great reminder of what you actually did. Let's face it, sometimes it is easy for us to forget or discount what we have done during the day as not a big deal. Since I am a list maker, I am always crossing things off my lists, which in itself is gratifying. I love getting to the end of a day and seeing all the little things that I've done and know that I put in some effort and made some progress in moving forward.

If you make lists during the day, doing it again at night might feel redundant, but like most writing exercises, this will help solidify in your mind that you did indeed accomplish something that mattered. Writing that list is satisfying and just brings the journey of change to a whole new level, and it doesn't take a lot of time either. Sometimes it can be as simple as making a list like the following.

Tuesday
Ate healthy
Worked out
Didn't impulse buy at the store

Encouraged a friend
Made a sale
Wrote 500 words
Read 15 pages
Spent time with spouse

You get the idea. This list could include a multitude of things from a variety of areas of your life, including your health, fitness, career, family, money, education, or even your social life. There are so many little things a person can do every day to change their lives in significant ways, and taking the time to acknowledge those steps, that daily effort, is important. Doing this exercise is a great thing to add to your daily activity because it reinforces that effort in your mind and reminds you of what you have accomplished.

It will help you wake up in the morning feeling like you can face another day, that you can take that step into the future and tackle the little things that need to be done in order to get you where you want to be. And sometimes taking the time to note the good things that happened on that day is even more important when life gets hard, complicated, challenging and frustrating. And you know we all have those days, right? No one is exempt from the hard days that get under our skin, and the problems could come from anywhere and anyone. Something or someone gets to us, and suddenly our mood changes. We find ourselves in a negative headspace wishing things were different, hoping things will change, angry at the world or something else. We get stuck in those swirling thoughts and end up losing focus on the good that happened that day, the things we accomplished.

That is why doing this activity is so important. It is so easy to get into a negative place and remain there too long. It is natural to let the frustrating things that happen to us in the day get in the way of the good and change our focus. And not to mention change how we treat the people around us, which isn't fair to anyone.

Celebrating the big milestones, the little benchmarks and steps that you do each day to get to the next level, are not just important, they are vital.

It is also important to share your journey with others and let them help you celebrate your successes as you go through the process. And let them lift you up when you struggle. You know who is on your side, who cherishes you and wants you to succeed. You know who you can trust to be on your side and support your journey. You know who can see the reason to celebrate both the big and small things. Such people do exist. Whether you choose to share these things with a group of people or one individual, it is going to help you on your journey.

I am so blessed to have people like this in my corner. I have friends who know what I struggle with and celebrate with me when I achieve something that might not be as significant to someone else. They share my journey with me, and I am so grateful for that. Having people in your corner to cheer you on through the good and the bad, the big and the small, is going to encourage you and push you closer to the goals you want to accomplish. And in return, you have the opportunity to do the same thing for them. You have the chance to help them achieve goals and see their dreams become a reality.

People who understand these journeys of change and personal growth are generally people who want the same thing in their own life. They appreciate your journey and the effort you are putting in because they understand what it takes, and they care for you. And supporting their journey, their dreams, and their plans for change does not take away from your own.

Supporting the people you care about, and even strangers for that matter, doesn't make what you are doing less productive, less important, or less meaningful. It seems like in this day and age, it is easy to feel like if you boost or encourage others, they will somehow surpass you or you will end up feeling like "less than" for some reason. The opposite is true. Boosting others, in fact, boosts your life, your productivity, and your attitude. So it's worth encouraging. Plus, it feels good, doesn't it? It feels great to celebrate not just ourselves but others as well.

Celebrating your efforts and acknowledging your accomplishments, regardless of the size, will boost your confidence. It will allow you to see yourself in a new light and help you realize that you are indeed capable of change. It will help you see that you are worth the effort too, because you are. You may not see yourself as strong or capable. You may question your ability to achieve goals or change your life. I understand that feeling so much. However, it is not true. For you or me.

When you celebrate yourself, you are essentially giving yourself an idea of how to up the ante as you go forward. Did you reach a goal? Great! Now you have a chance to raise the bar and take it a step further.

Celebrating your accomplishments is a chance for you to recognize what you are succeeding in. And when you can see it, others can see it too.

When you don't appreciate your journey and the successes you have, you are downplaying the accomplishments and headway you are making. Would you allow a friend to do that? Would you let someone you care about to act or talk like what they have achieved doesn't matter? Of course not! You would tell them how great they are, or what a fantastic job they are doing. You would congratulate them and ask them what is next on their list of goals.

Why aren't you doing that for yourself? Why is it sometimes so hard to grasp the idea that celebrating our achievements isn't always about ego or thinking we are somehow better than others? It can be taken to that extreme, no doubt, but being able to acknowledge your accomplishments is a healthy thing to do, and when you do that you are boosting your ability to take things further. Your ability to learn and grow more. You are increasing your ability to see what is working and why it is working. And you are making it more possible for you to positively impact the lives of others around you, and that is very valuable.

You are capable of change, you are capable of creating a new life for yourself, and you are capable of growing, learning, and becoming a better person. When you choose to celebrate the things you achieve and overcome, you will begin to see your worth and abilities much more clearly. And over time, you will begin to truly believe in yourself.

Your efforts matter and should be celebrated. Your milestones and benchmarks matter and when you reach those, they should be celebrated.

You should be celebrated.

Chapter review:

Celebrate and acknowledge the effort you are putting into changing your life.

Sometimes asking yourself questions about what you have accomplished that day can open your mind to the truth and help you see what you are truly accomplishing, even if it feels like you are only treading water.

If you are making an effort, if you are trying, if you are doing what you can to take steps forward, there is something to be proud of yourself for, something to celebrate. Guaranteed.

Supporting the goals and dreams the other people in your life have doesn't make what you are doing less productive, less important, and less meaningful.

Celebrating your efforts and acknowledging your accomplishments, regardless of the size, will boost your confidence. It will allow you to see yourself in a new light and help you realize that you are indeed capable of change.

Take action challenge!

Celebrate challenge? Who's with me?!

This is one of my favorite challenges, and one of my favorite things to do every day! It is so easy for us to get to the end of the day and think that we didn't accomplish anything or that we didn't get any closer to our goals that day. This activity can help you refocus and see if you are choosing actions that will get you closer to your goals.

What I want you to do is take out a sheet of paper and a pen and place it on your nightstand. For the next seven days, just after you crawl into bed, write down three things you did that day to improve your life. Did you eat right? Save money? Exercise? Invest in a relationship or friendship? Make a sale? Write a few words? There could be so many different things you could list here.

Commit yourself to doing this for a full seven days. I think you'll see how powerful it can be and that there is much to celebrate!

Take action now!

Joy is what happens to us when we allow ourselves to recognize how good things really are.

~ Marianne Williamson

CHAPTER 10

CHOOSE JOY

When it comes to the topic of change, you can't discuss it without commenting on joy. Well, I can't at least. Change is hard. I have probably said it a million times by now, but it is true. We all have things that we do every day that we want to change, and how many times have we tried to change them? How many times have we tried to change bad habits, or create new good ones, only to find ourselves back where we started? Do you have a desire to do something different, to become a better person or to learn a new skill, and you just never seem to find yourself back in that place? I know I've done it so many times myself. I have started out on a journey, only to find myself in the same place again and again, and it's frustrating!

You get derailed, you get distracted, and you get discouraged. That is just how life is at times. It is impossible to avoid frustrations and roadblocks like this from happening completely. I wish that weren't the case, but you know it's true. You cannot avoid the hard things in life, but you can choose your attitude about them. You can choose how you view the world, the situation at hand and the people around you. You can choose your attitude.

You can choose joy.

Any journey that includes change isn't always a happy one; I have no doubt we can all agree upon that. If it was, I am sure more people would pursue it themselves and be more consistent about making an effort toward it than they are. However, that does not mean that the journey has to be one of total struggle and frustration, but it will be if we choose it to be or allow it to be.

When it comes to joy, it doesn't have to mean that we're smiling all the time or that we are laughing and jumping around with excitement. It seems that at times, we think of joy as this outward expression of happiness or exuberance. And that is true at certain points of our journey; there are those moments of joy that come out with a yell, happy tears, or laughter. We shouldn't feel like we are not capable of joy because we are not acting a certain way. Joy doesn't have to look that way, and I think that is something we need to acknowledge.

Joy doesn't have to be a big show. Joy can be simple and quiet.

A person can feel joy, happiness, and exuberance without waving their arms in the air or making some grand announcement. Joy can be felt when you have a moment of peace and quiet or when you make someone else smile. You can find the joy in sipping a cup of coffee for a few minutes in silence, closing your eyes and listening to your favorite music, or while cuddling with your significant other on the couch while you watch a movie.

CHOOSE CHANGE

Just like we can choose our attitude, we can choose joy. We can choose happiness. We can decide to see our successes and our abilities to achieve our goals in the good and the bad.

Choose to find joy in the little things you accomplish, the little steps forward you take. Choose joy when you achieve a tiny piece of a goal or take some step forward that you have never done before. It doesn't have to be big. It doesn't even have to be something anyone else will notice. Find joy in those little things. Celebrate those, because when you do, your life will be dramatically changed for the better.

I just wrote about 1000 words before going in to work today. Although it's not anything monumental or record-breaking, it is a step forward to one of my goals, and I am thankful for that. That little piece of my day gives me joy, lately. I have been struggling to find the happiness in a lot of areas of my life. I have been discouraged with where I am in life in some ways, but writing those thousand words is a step forward in the right direction for me. And today, I chose to be joyful about that. That action changed my perspective on the day and will carry me through whatever frustrations come my way today at the office.

And with joy comes laughter, one of my favorite things in life.

Laughter is so powerful. It feels so good when we laugh really hard, doesn't it? Don't you just feel so much better after having a good laugh? A small laugh or a big laugh affects your entire body in such a positive way.

Dr. Lee Berk and Dr. Stanley Tan, two researchers out of California, looked into the benefits of laughter and found that laughter is something that can lower your blood pressure, reduce stress levels, improve your heart health, trigger endorphins to be released in your body, and improve a person's "sense of well-being," not to mention that it works your abs.[11] (Bonus! Bring on that laughter, please!) Those are all such amazing benefits for our bodies and lives, and they are all achieved by the simple and joyful act of laughter. That just makes me even more compelled to point out how important choosing joy and choosing to laugh really are.

How can we deny ourselves of that?

I can't tell you how many times I have felt relief from just the simple act of laughter when things have been intense, frustrating or painful. Sometimes it happens at the most inopportune time. I think we've all been through that before, when you're in a situation that isn't funny at all but something strikes your funny bone, and you can't help yourself but let it out.

Being someone who struggles with depression and anxiety on various levels during different seasons of life, laughter is something that has helped me push through many of the difficult things that have happened.

Laughter is one of those things that can carry you through the bad times and allow you to feel human when things get hard. It also makes the good times even better.

One of the things I get the most comments about when people meet me or get to know me is my laugh. I'm assuming that is a good thing and that their comments are meant to be a compliment. I am grateful that it is something that is very prevalent about my personality. I know I can be reserved at times, being an introvert and all, but I am glad that when people meet me, they can see that joy in me. That is the type of person I want to be. I want to choose joy, and I work hard to do that.

My ability to find joy in the little things, to be able to laugh so easily and so much, is something that I cherish. It allows me to let go of frustrations or sadness so much faster, to become frustrated less often, and to feel much less stress. Why would I want to give that up?

Not everyone is going to be too keen on your choice to choose joy, whether you are in the process of changing your life or not. It is hard for some to understand why a person would make such an effort in certain circumstances. I once worked a production job that I didn't enjoy too much, but the people I worked with were so much fun. It was a great group, and though the work wasn't always fun, we made a point of enjoying our days. We also noticed that on the days we had fun, our output numbers were much higher than the days we were quiet and kept to ourselves. The people made all the difference there, and it really seemed as though they all wanted to enjoy their days, too. Well, except for our manager. There came a point where my manager decided he needed to tell me he didn't like me. His reason? He said I was too happy. Can you believe he actually said that? I don't feel like I am generally annoying with my happiness; I could be wrong, I guess, but I don't feel like on a normal day I am over the top about it. I just work hard to find the joy in my day and a reason to laugh. His reaction to me was not something I was expecting in the least, but there are people out there who just cannot handle someone who tries to see the good in the day. I want to be the same person at home, out in public, and at work. Needless to say, after that conversation with my manager, my productivity dwindled, and it ultimately led to me leaving the job in just a few short weeks. (And so did a lot of other people!) Life is too short to spend forty hours a week being around someone like that.

Laughter is something that can help reduce the stress that comes with the process. Changing what you are doing, your direction and your habits is a lot of work. It can take its toll on you, so making a point to find the joy and laughter and enjoy the moments you have been given is something that is going to make the journey that much more enjoyable and beneficial.

We have already talked about what impact others have on our journey of change, how their comments and their reactions to what we are doing can be hard to deal with. Even though we have had some discussion about this already, I think it is important to cover it again, because we all have a connection to individuals who cannot seem to find their way out of a gloomy fog. Negative people steal joy, and it is hard not to succumb to the negativity they bring into your life when you are surrounded by it. These people are pessimistic, gloomy and cynical about everything that happens to them or around them. Every comment out of their mouth has some tinge of negativity to it, no matter what the subject.

When you are around someone like that on a regular basis, it is hard not to adopt their reactions or attitude as your own without some plan of action or support system to help you deal with it. Many people that are like this that cannot seem to find the joy in the day-to-day life they live and are not going to be receptive to a positive attitude or attempts to change their outlook. If they are going to change, it is going to be something they are going to have to embrace for themselves.

They need to come to the realization in some way on their own. You might be able to lead them to that place by living a certain way, but you cannot force it on them. You cannot force them to change. That means in the meantime, you have to come up with a plan so you can hold onto your joy, to find ways and reasons to laugh throughout your day, and avoid becoming someone you don't want to be by default.

Take the time to praise them for something positive they have done. Don't waste time debating things with them that don't really matter. Help them when you have a chance. Choose topics of conversation that are light and won't get you into a negative place with them, avoiding things that trigger them to go to negative places in conversation. We all have those, so be aware of what they are for others. If they constantly have negative comments, acknowledge some with a positive twist in some way, and ignore others. Don't acknowledge every negative comment they have with something positive. Otherwise, you are going to end up driving them crazy and potentially putting a wedge between you and them.

The most important thing to remember here is to be responsible for your reaction. Be in control of your attitude. You are the one who is responsible for finding the joy in your day, finding reasons to laugh and finding ways to be positive. That lies on your shoulders, no matter what is going on in your life. As I'm writing this, I am saying it out loud to myself. I am responsible for making this day count, for choosing actions that move me forward, and for finding the good in the day and in the people who are around me regardless of how they are acting.

What brings you joy? What are the sources of joy? I really hope that it is not a question you have to spend a lot of time thinking about in order to find an answer. I hope that something comes to your mind pretty easily as you read it. I hope you have access to a great deal of joy.

My family is at the top of the list. I am the proud aunt of four gorgeous nieces who are a lot of fun to be around. They work hard to make me laugh, and I appreciate their effort so much. I enjoy spending time with them. Just seeing their smiling faces brings my heart joy. I'm very close to my parents as well, and the amount of time we have spent laughing together is precious to me. The same goes with friends. Most of the people I'm closest to do not live in the same town as I do, which isn't terribly convenient all the time, but thankfully with all the technology available to us, we can stay in close touch and still enjoy each other's day-to-day lives. Those friendships are something I cherish deeply.

Having a community of friends and family is something that can be a source of joy and a source of laughter as well. It is not something we should take for granted in any way.

Focusing energy on activities, hobbies and work activities that alleviate the pressures and stress that change brings helps a person keep their joy during the process. Obviously, writing is high on my list. Photography is another big one for me. Being able to get out into the country and find a serene landscape to photograph, noticing something on the street that strikes me interesting at random, or even taking portraits for someone is a great way for me to de-stress, and it triggers something in my brain that makes me happy. Sometimes looking through that lens helps me either find a new perspective or put things in perspective.

There are certain things that I love about everyday life, everyday experiences, like looking up at the sky to see what the clouds look like. I always notice when I stop doing this on a regular basis. When I stop observing the world around me, I'm spending too much time looking down at the ground and not focusing on possibilities as much. I also enjoy watching the sunset each night from my kitchen table as I am writing or working on projects. I get all giddy watching the sky change colors, and it is different every night. Other simple pleasures that can bring a person joy could be enjoying hot showers, lounging in comfy pajamas, looking at the stars, going to a concert, or whatever fits your personality and your way of recuperating.

Finding that source of joy, finding a reason to laugh or smile, and finding those pleasures that keep you going when life gets hard is so important. Having such things in your life makes it easier to step forward and do what you need to do to change your life. If you don't have that right now, I encourage you to find it, and if you do have that I urge you to step into it more.

Joy is so amazing. Choose it.

Chapter review:

You can choose how you view the world, the situation at hand and the people around you. You can choose your attitude.

Joy doesn't have to be a big show. Joy can be simple and quiet.

You cannot force people to see the joy in life like you do. It is something they have to embrace for themselves.

It is up to you to come up with a plan to hold onto your joy, to find ways and reasons to laugh throughout your day, so you don't become someone you don't want to be by default.

You are responsible for making this day count, for making mature choices that move you forward, for finding the good in the day and in the people that you are around, regardless of how they are acting.

Take action challenge!

You up for another challenge?

We all have someone in our lives that brings us down in some way, whether they mean to or not. Those kinds of relationships are challenging and frustrating and can really become a burden to bear. Whether you are in that place right now or not, I want you to start thinking about how you can deal with those people in your life. It is important to have a game plan on how you are going to keep your joy when you are around people who seem determined to bring you down. That is what I want to challenge you to do right now. This isn't always an easy task, but it is an important one.

The best way to figure out how to deal with this situation is to ask yourself some questions. Why is this person acting this way? Why are they treating me like this? Am I doing something to make the situation worse? Am I encouraging it somehow? Is this something I can talk to them about? From there, you can formulate a plan on how you can approach this person and situation in the best way. Don't assume every tack you take will work with every person. It is important for you to do this on a person-to-person basis. Start writing down some ideas you have! And take action!

Take action now!

The secret of your future is hidden in your daily routine.

~ Mike Murdock

CHAPTER 11

ROUTINE POWER

Setting up a routine can be extremely helpful and ultimately get you further much faster. Routines can feel restricting at times, but the truth is that if they are used correctly, they have the potential to expedite your results and make your life blast off.

You need to realize that just like the plans we make, routines also need to be dynamic. As life happens, as plans change, as responsibilities and situations arise in our lives, routines we have may need adjusting as well. Life changes are some of those things in life we can count on, and to make the most of the change, we need to change with it. And that includes changing our routines.

We are all creatures of habit to some degree, so this can be challenging. We can get stuck in our ways and like the system we have created. Routines should be fluid, as life is ever changing just like our plans should be. You may need to adjust the time you get up or what time you crawl into bed. You may need to work out in the morning instead of at night or vice versa. You may need to change the hours you work, the days you work, or the amount of work you put in at your job.

Whatever it is, know that adjustments will need to be made to your daily routine in order to acclimate to the change that is occurring and keep you moving forward. It will keep you from losing momentum, and that is what I am hoping to help you with. Be willing to change your routine to accommodate the things that happen in your life and don't lose ground in your pursuit of change. This flexibility isn't always easy; for some of us, it's extra hard, but in the end, you will be glad you made that decision.

Just recently, we had a storm come through, and I made the decision to spend the night at my parents' house just as a precaution. It definitely threw off my plans for that evening and the next morning as well, but I adjusted as well as I could. I picked the most important things I needed to complete for each day and let everything else go. My schedule changed, but I didn't allow that to throw me completely off track. Afterward, it felt so great that I hadn't let the storm take me completely off course. I had achieved my priorities. I had kept my focus on what is important and continued on.

What can a good routine do for you in your pursuit of change? I am so glad you asked. A good routine can provide structure for your day. In other words, it can help you stay on track and help you be more productive. A routine is not something that has to dominate your entire day or your entire schedule. Well, unless that is something you want to do. (Which is the way I tend to lean, even though it never works out too well.) Setting aside a certain slot of time each day to work on a specific project and giving focused time to the things that are important to you will get you closer to your goals than if you say you are going to do those things "sometime that day." If you are anything like me, that time of day never comes. It is easy to get home from work and decide that you are not in the mood anymore or it doesn't feel as important at that moment so it can be put off until later. Whenever I take that attitude about the things I need to do, the result is always a feeling of regret. I should have followed through.

Routines can help you develop good habits and replace the ones you don't want anymore, the ones that keep you from growing as a person and achieving what you could accomplish. Sometimes it is hard to let those go. I know how much I kind of love my bad habits, but I don't want to cling to them and sacrifice the amazing things that could happen in my life. A person needs to make room in their life for the incredible. I want that (and more) for my life, and I want that for you too.

You have probably heard the saying that if you do the same thing you've always done, you are going to get what you have always gotten. Doing the same thing over and over and expecting something to change in your life is foolish. It is easy to get into that cycle, but we need to be more aware of our actions than that and understand that repeating bad decisions and bad choices or being irresponsible with our time, money and energy is only going to get us more of what we say we don't want. Our actions, our plans, and our routines need to match our desires and the goals we say we want to accomplish. If they don't match, we are not going to make a whole lot of progress. We are not going to get to the outcome we are hoping for. It is as simple as that. Yet, not always as simple to carry out sometimes.

That is why routines are so important when you are choosing to make changes to your life, big or small. The routines you carry out are going to either get you closer to the end goal or further away.

Routines are great when you are trying to improve your skills. Focused time on a specific skill set is necessary to take you from a mediocre level to the level of expert.

Making a point to put a routine into your week and taking the time to plan out your days gives you control over what you allow into your day. You attach value to a particular activity and are deliberate and intentional about those actions.

Having a routine and a plan for your day-to-day life means you are ultimately limiting procrastination. Do you ever put things off? Yeah, me too. "Later," I tell myself. "I'll do them later. I'll take care of it later." And a day goes by, then a week, and then maybe a month. Being intentional about a routine is going to help keep you from getting off track or putting things off. Setting time aside each morning to write has been one of the biggest changes for me when it comes to my writing routine. I know when I am going to get it done, I know it's scheduled into my day, and there isn't a question about whether I will sit down and do it or not. It is part of my day like my day job is. I have a routine, a schedule. That way, if I don't take the time to write after work or I get caught up in something else, I know that I have completed that activity already in its allotted time. The same rule applies to getting my workout completed each day.

Making a point of saying to yourself that "this is important enough to me to set aside a specific time of the day to focus on it" is a big step in moving forward and changing our life. When you are saying that something is important to you, that it matters enough to make it a priority, you are solidifying in your mind that this is vital to you. You are telling yourself that this particular thing is non-negotiable and something you don't want to compromise on.

One of the most impactful routines I have added into my life is The Miracle Morning. If you have not read this book, I urge you to pick it up. In it, Hal Elrod discusses his journey of change after the economic crash in 2007. He was struggling and finally reached out to a friend to confess his situation and get some help. Through this journey, he created a morning routine that turned into a book, which has truly turned into a movement. The subtitle of the book is "the not-so-obvious secret guaranteed to transform your life (before 8 AM)." And how true that is.

The steps, called the SAVERS, are done each day before 8 AM: Silence, Affirmations, Visualizations, Exercising, Reading, and Scribing (his word for writing).[12] Making this a daily practice, even just one minute of each, can propel your life into places you never expected. Being part of The Miracle Morning Community online, I have seen so many people change their lives in just a short amount of time.

Because of this routine that I have added to my life, I have become more committed to my goals, more positive and focused on the things that impact my life. And I spend less time on the things that don't get me anywhere at all.

Creating routines and setting aside special times to work on projects will save you from wasted time as well. This, of course, is along the same lines as procrastination, but sometimes the wasted time isn't something we do intentionally. We can get caught up in what is going on around us.

We can waste time by focusing on things that don't matter or activities that take our time and energy but don't move us forward.

I don't know about you, but I occasionally get the feeling of guilt when I waste time. I have a hard time getting to the end of a day and realizing that I could have done so much more, that there could have been more accomplished.

I am not suggesting that you shouldn't relax. I am also not saying you should pack so much into a day that you don't have time to breathe. Busy and productive days are amazing (at least I think so), but if you enjoy days that are busy like that, make sure you take the time to relax and recuperate in a way that recharges you. Some people recharge by being around people, and some people (like me) recharge by spending time alone. Whichever is best suited for you, make sure you take the time to do that so you don't burn out. When a person reaches the point of burning out, it can often lead to the individual getting off track for a long period of time. Or just flat out giving up. There is only so much a person can handle, so don't risk the possibility of giving up or falling off track by taking on so much you just quit. Make time for resting, relaxing, recuperating and recharging. They are vital in your pursuit of changing your life, so don't disregard their value.

If you want to make your dreams a reality, you should prioritize what matters to you. You should set up routines to keep you on track and to move you forward. It isn't always the easiest, but if it matters enough to you, you will find a way to do it. Instead of wasting time and making excuses and wishing for things, make it happen. It is a better use of your energy and time.

When you accomplish something, doesn't it feel fantastic? Don't you feel like you have conquered the world somehow? Even if it is something small, it gives you a boost of confidence. That sense of accomplishment feels great and is so satisfying. And the truth is, when you get that feeling once, you are going to want it again and again. The hope is that those activities that give you those positive feelings end up part of your regular routine.

If you follow the routine you have set up for yourself, if you embrace the changes you need to make in order to move forward and do what needs to be done, that sense of accomplishment will be addictive.

When you fall out of the routine and don't make things happen the way you should, it can be hard to deal with. Not following through on the things you had planned for the day isn't the end of the world. It isn't, though it can feel like it sometimes. Not following through on what you intended to can feel like you've failed. Trust me, you haven't. Although, if you continue to let your routine, your plans, and your time go to waste and don't follow through on what you need to do, you are letting opportunities pass you by.

It may not feel like a big deal at the time, that you aren't losing anything by putting things off. You may not even notice in the short term, but the truth is, after a while your life is going to end up somewhere you never intended it to go, and you will notice.

Routine is what gets you from where you are now to where you want to be. A routine is what is going to get you from the life you have to the life you want. A routine is the ticket to success and achievement of your goals.

Please remember, the routine you choose doesn't have to be complicated. I don't have this expectation that you will completely overhaul your schedule and fill up every second of every day. That just isn't realistic. A routine can be as simple as adding a half hour of writing to your day for the book you want to publish, squeezing in a twenty-minute workout to help boost your health, or finding ten minutes at the end of the day to plan the following day. There are so many small actions that can take you a step further from where you are and closer to where you want to be.

What small thing can be done in order to get you closer to your goal? Are you saving money, trying to get healthier, looking into new career options, or taking steps to better your social life and relationships? Whatever it is you are hoping to become better at, however you are trying to improve your life, it can be done over time with small changes that you do continually. It can be done when you build a routine for yourself.

I know there are some people who aren't in love with planning and routines like I am. For some, setting up routines, making lists and following a plan is not the most exciting thing in the world. There are some who prefer to live by the seat of their pants and let life happen without a whole lot of planning. Some people find enjoyment in that way of living, which is great. Spontaneity is an awesome thing, and it can bring a lot of joy to someone's life. Though I am not the most spontaneous person myself, it brings a certain amount of excitement to my life when it happens. Though living that way on a regular basis doesn't suit me personally, I see the value in it.

However, it doesn't matter if you are more on the spontaneous side or if you are a planner, because a routine is something that can benefit someone on either side of the coin. You don't have to be one or the other to take advantage of what a routine can do for your life. Don't just assume that if you are one or the other that you can't utilize this tool. It is a universal mechanism, and it is such a great asset to create a new life. *Your* new life.

Growing pains come with any change you go through. I have realized this more and more as I have been going through the process of change myself. I have been trying to adjust to a new schedule, new expectations, and new goals. It is all so new to me, and it hasn't gone flawlessly. I have struggled as I have been integrating some huge goals into my life.

There is going to be a period of adjustment when things feel hard and frustrating, and you are tempted to give up. You may feel like the change is impossible and that the new routines you are setting up for yourself are too complicated or too impossible. You may start thinking that you are better off staying where you are and not trying anymore, that the effort isn't worth the energy, or that you aren't worth the fight. This is where you need to keep pressing forward. This is where you need to continue following your plan and focusing on your new routine.

When you have been living one way for a long period of time, sometimes it is hard to change. It can be a bumpy start when you begin to adjust your life and set up a new routine, so don't expect it to go perfectly from the get-go.

I am reminded of something I read in Jeff Goin's book, *You Are a Writer*. Though the book is about the creative life, I feel like the following statement hits home when it comes to the truth about the beginning stages of changing your life and setting up a routine.

Professional weight lifters don't get sore like you and I do when we lift weights. They show up, push themselves, build muscle, and go home. Then tomorrow, they get up and do it again. The less they think, the more successful they are. The same is true of any craft. Soreness is the result of the untrained muscle. If you practice every day, you don't get fatigued. All muscles are built this way, even creative ones. If you do anything long enough, it becomes habitual.[13]

Don't let up. The soreness you feel isn't because you aren't capable, and it isn't because you aren't worthy. It is because you haven't been consistent with making the choices you need to make in order to step forward into your goals. If you lose a day, give yourself some grace, but don't let it turn into two days. Pressing on can be hard to do. You can get that feeling that tells you it is time to give up, surrender to what is and not try to go any further. Fighting these thoughts and feelings is tough, but you need to realize that this is temporary. As time goes on and you push through and do those new routines you have set up for yourself, you are going to get past this point.

The other thing you need to realize is that every time you give up on your plan or routine, every time you don't follow through or you take time off from putting effort into your goals, you will have to go through those growing pains again. You will have to retrain those muscles all over again. Every time you restart your plan, every time you start and stop, you have to go through these same emotions and the roller coaster that comes along with it. Isn't that enough of a reason to stop giving up and taking time off? If you are sick of starting over, stop quitting.

Routines can be the tool that gets you where you want to go. Changing a particular area of your life and setting aside specific time to improve or acquire a new skill can mean the difference between making your dreams happen or watching your life become something that you never intended it to be. You have the choice to utilize the things that will help you get from where you are to where you want to be.

What are you going to do?

Chapter review:

Setting aside a particular slot of time each day to work on a specific project and giving focused time to the things that are important to you will get you closer to your goals than if you say you are going to do those things "sometime that day."

Routines can help you develop good habits and replace the ones you don't want in your life anymore, the ones that keep you from growing and achieving what you could accomplish.

Your actions, your plans, and your routines need to match your desires and the things you say you want to do.

When you are making changes to your life, there will be growing pains and a period of adjustment to push through.

Every time you give up on your plan and your routine, every time you don't follow through or you take time off from putting effort into your goals, you will have to go through the growing pains all over again.

Take action challenge!

You guessed it! Challenge time!

What I want you to do is choose something you want to improve on or a skill you want to acquire. What is something you want to add to your life? What skill are you lacking? What activity do you want or need to spend more time on, either for fun or productivity? I am going to leave this open for you to decide because ultimately, this needs to fit into the life you want to create for yourself.

Now, set aside a half hour every day for this one particular thing you have chosen to do. It can be in the morning, afternoon or evening. The timing doesn't matter as much as the follow-through. You know when you are at your best to complete it, and you also know when you have time for it. Spend a half hour each day for seven days and see what happens. The more you do it, the more results you will see.

Take action now!

*Sometimes asking for help is the bravest move you can make.
You don't have to go it alone.*

CHAPTER 12

ASK FOR HELP

None of us are going to have all the answers for every situation that comes our way as we go through the process of changing our lives. I know, I know, it isn't fun to read that sentence, but you know it is the truth. There is not one person on this planet who knows how to deal with every situation or every type of person that is out there. There is not one person who can do it alone. It sure would be nice sometimes, but we are just not built that way. And as we will discuss, there is good reason for that.

This is the part of the process that I struggle with more than any others, I have to admit. It is difficult for me to tell you that asking for help and reaching out for assistance is something that I have struggled with for a very long time. However, it is 100 percent the truth.

I don't think I am terribly vain, have a massive ego, or that I have all the answers. I don't think I am someone who doesn't need help or advice from time to time. I think my desire to be able to do things on my own without asking for any kind of help stems from a period of time in my life when I was surviving only because of the support I was getting from other people. Without that help, I would have drowned, and I don't know how I would have made it through. During that time, all I wanted was to be able to take care of myself. My big dream in life was to be able to pay my own bills. That was all I cared about. I wanted to be able to fend for myself, pay my way in life and not have someone else doing the things I should be able to do for myself.

I was an adult, after all. I wanted my independence. And not only that, I wanted my pride back. I wanted some dignity. I don't think I was without those attributes when I was struggling so much back then; however, I felt like I was a burden on others, particularly my family. I didn't like it, and I never wanted to feel that way again. I never wanted to look at myself in the mirror knowing that someone else was doing things for me that I should be doing for myself. My independence was my focus. And, in all honesty, it is still that way in many respects.

I have a hard time asking someone to help me. I have a hard time showing that I need it. I don't want to be a burden to anyone. I don't want people to feel like they have to carry me. I don't want to feel like I am putting more pressure on someone or bringing something negative into their life. And I don't like looking or feeling incapable.

My independence runs deep, so accepting the truth that I need to reach out is not always the easiest. What truth am I speaking of?

That asking for help does not make a person weak.

It is, in fact, the opposite. Your decision to reach out and seek assistance is a sign of strength. And I can tell you that I am always better off when I do it. I know that if I forge ahead when I don't know what I am doing, I risk looking foolish and it has the potential of blowing up in my face later on, which I don't want. The landmines and issues you avoid when you swallow your pride and ask for help can be massive.

For the past year or so, I have been thinking about asking someone to mentor me. I knew I needed it. I wanted it, but I couldn't seem to get myself to take that step and reach out. It took me a year after deciding who I wanted to ask to actually contact the person. It was so hard to do, even though I knew the person would more than likely be receptive to it. I felt anxious when I pressed send on my long email to them, and as hard as it was to ask, I am so glad I did. My life has been ever changed for the better since that initial contact. I knew there were things I needed to improve on and get help with, things that were out of my depth without some guidance and encouragement.

It isn't always easy to ask for help. Maybe you struggle with it like I do, even if not quite as much, or more perhaps. What I do know is that the resistance to asking for help is built into each of us to some degree. Maybe it is in a specific area of your life, or over one particular topic. I don't know what it is for you that makes asking for help hard to do, but I can tell you something for certain.

You are better off when you open your mouth and ask for what you need than if you choose to keep quiet and let things fester inside of you. Situations can build up into bigger things in your life than they ever had to be.

Asking others for help is an amazing and special thing. You know the people in your life care so much for you. Your friends and family want what is best for you. Though they might not understand your goals and the changes you are making, they want to support you, to lift you up and to encourage you.

When you are making changes and making efforts to become a better version of yourself, the people around you might not know how to support you. If you are doing something they have never done or dreamed of, they may not know how to encourage you in your journey. Remember, we talked about giving some grace to those who don't understand and being patient with the fact that they may not be able to comprehend the reason you feel this is necessary. Giving those people grace is important, and on that same note, you also need to share how they can help you. Let them have their reactions and allow them to feel what they need to feel when you initially share your plans with them.

Then follow that up with some helpful tips for them. How can they help you? What can they do to support you, if anything? Do you need them to pitch in with the process in some way? Or do you just need the people in your life to acknowledge your goal, your dream, your passion, and simply tell you that they are behind you no matter what? Sometimes that is all a person needs.

Do you have that? Is that something you want on your journey of change?

Quite often, people don't know what you want from them, what you need from them, or how they can better support you. They want to, but they are unsure of what that entails or what that looks like, especially if you are on a journey they don't understand. Share with them, express your needs to them. They love you, they care for you. They want to see you succeed, they want to help you get to the next level, so let them help you. They may feel like they are supporting you and if they knew they weren't actually helping you, they would feel so guilty. Show them how they can make a positive impact on your life.

I should note that when you start expressing these needs people, hinting about it probably won't get you very far. They may not be able to decipher the signals you are sending out. They might just think you are acting a little weird, to be honest, but you need to understand that making concrete statements rather than just dropping hints is going to get you a lot further a lot faster.

It rarely works for me to throw out hints, hoping the other person will catch on to what I am trying to say. Don't waste your time with that when it comes to such an important subject. Most of the time, approaching people that way misuses time and just gets you frustrated and leaves them confused. Don't do that to yourself, or to them.

How can the people in your life be better friends to you? I am sure they would want to know! Wouldn't you? Let's reverse the situation here for a second. If a friend of yours was chasing after a goal, trying to change their life in some positive way, wouldn't you want them to be able to come to you and ask if you could help them in a certain way? Wouldn't you want them to let you know if something you are doing is hurting their progress or discouraging them in some way? If it is something you would want to know from them, chances are they would want you to share that with them as well. You want to be a good friend to them, you want them to be able to approach you and ask for help and encouragement. Your friends are hoping you feel the same way with them.

I recently had a friend of mine say to me that I needed to start telling the people in my life what I need from them. She was right. She told me that I needed to tell her what I needed from her to get me closer to my goals. She also said I needed to tell the other people in my life how they can better help me get to where I want to be. She ended with the following, which made me tear up a bit.

You are super independent, and it's probably crippling you when things get heavy and overwhelming. There's a time to share the burden, and there's a lot of people who would love to do that.

Being the independent person I am, I want to be able to carry things alone and not be a burden for someone else. To not add to someone else's plate. I would prefer to take on their load than share my own. For whatever reason, that is how I am wired, and it is always a battle to do things any differently. But I need to, and I should. As you should, too.

Sharing your goals, easing your burdens, and asking for help and encouragement are things that bring people closer together. Sharing these parts of ourselves is something that connects us to each other in deeper ways. If you want a shallow relationship, keep things to yourself. Don't share, don't invest. If your goal is to be so independent that you keep everything to yourself, on yourself, and hold all your troubles and struggles to yourself, the truth is you are going to end up quite alone and with a whole mess of burdens to carry. I don't know about you, but that is not what I want for my life.

I think one of the biggest turning points in my adult life came when I started to share what was going on in my life with people I could trust. I don't know exactly when I started to share more, or when I really started to trust people more, but I know over time I realized how much it mattered and how much it helped me. I felt closer to other people because of it. I think that has been the biggest blessing in my life, having people that I can trust with my heart and my thoughts, who encourage me when things are tough or talk me through when life feels confusing or frustrating. I have been blessed with amazing friends, and I pray that they know how much I appreciate them and that I am here for them no matter what!

Admitting that you need help from someone—that you don't know it all—is not always the easiest thing to do. It is kind of a blow to the ego at times, but the benefits are so numerous and wonderful, you are just better off asking. Not only will you get further faster, getting closer to your goal and making more progress toward changing your life, but you will also learn something new and deepen relationships in the process. How is that a bad thing?

I want to encourage you to step out of your comfort zone and reach out to someone for help. What is it you are looking to change about your life? What are you struggling with? And who can you trust to give you good advice or just be a listening ear? Sometimes having someone listen is all a person needs. Think about who you have in your life and who would be a safe person to start with.

When it comes to being in a relationship, I am no expert. I've been single for a very long time, so I am not going to start spouting out a bunch of relationship advice here. However, I do feel like it is important to broach the subject here a little bit. When it comes to sharing your needs and wants with another person, I want to emphasize the importance of doing this with your spouse. Your significant other cannot read your mind any more than anyone else. It is important to make sure the communication between you is solid, that you are sharing your life together and working through things together.

I know every relationship is different, but when you are committed to each other, there should be a higher level of communication between you. You should be able to share what you need in the relationship, what will help you, and what you are hoping for. And they should be able to do the same.

Asking for help, sharing your burdens, and telling the people that you need specific things from them are all parts of a healthy relationship and friendship. You are not meant to go through life alone. You are not meant to go through the process of changing your life alone. You are meant to be part of a community of people. That does not mean it needs to be a big one. It does not mean you need to have a large group of friends that you hang out with all the time. What it does mean, though, is that you are meant to go through life with people, sharing life with each other. The good and the bad.

Swallow your pride, set aside your fear, and realize that the people in your life want to be there for you. They care about you. Ask for help, tell people what you need from them in the relationship.

And make sure you offer to do the same for them in return.

Chapter review:

Asking for help does not make a person weak.

You are better off when you open your mouth and ask for what you need than if you choose to keep quiet and let things fester inside of you or allow situations to build up into bigger things in your life than they ever had to be.

You want your friends to ask you for help when they need it, right? They want the same from you.

Sharing your goals, easing your burdens, and asking for help and encouragement are all things that bring people closer together. Sharing those parts of ourselves is something that connects us to each other in deeper ways. If you want a shallow relationship, keep things to yourself.

You are not meant to go through life alone. You are not meant to go through the process of changing your life alone. You are meant to be a part of a community of people.

Take action challenge!

Woo hoo! Challenge time!

When we are looking to grow as people or in our skills, asking for help is always part of that picture. We can learn things on our own by reading or observing, but truthfully, connecting to another person just ups the ante and impacts our lives even more. This challenge right here is something that took me over a year to do myself. I thought about it and thought about it and finally stepped out of my comfort zone, and honestly, I wish I wouldn't have waited so long! It is time to ask for help.

Do you want a mentor? Do you want someone to help you learn a skill, talk you through tough situations or help you become a better leader? Who could be that person for you?

Take some time to think about what it is you need help with and who could help you with it, then approach them. Don't put it off for as long as I did. You know what you need, and I'm betting they will be willing to help you. Step out and ask for help!

Take action now!

Be bold, push yourself, and get comfortable being uncomfortable.

~ Angie Gels

CHAPTER 13

GET RADICAL

Throughout the process of writing this book, there has been this nagging thought in the back of my mind. This thought that something might be missing, from both the book and the journey itself. I tried to ignore it as best I could since the answer never seemed to be clear to me. I wanted to forget it because if it wasn't clear what was missing, the fact that it could be true was just plain annoying. I wasn't sure how to figure it out.

However, one day it hit me. Like one of those crystal-clear thoughts that just smack you in the face as if you should have seen it all along.

I thought: it is time to get radical.

What that meant exactly, I wasn't sure at the moment, but I knew the thought would follow me around for a while until I figured it out.

Approaching your life in a new way requires you to step out of your norm. What that means is that at times you need to be willing to step out of your normal routine, habits and comfort zone to challenge yourself a little. Or a lot. It can sound a little scary, but to make the changes we want to see in our lives, we are required to do something we don't normally do. It is so easy for me to say this to you, but I know it is not always easy to do. I struggle with it myself, but what I can tell you is that there is a benefit in taking these kinds of steps in your journey. There are advantages to taking a new approach. Sometimes you can't see it while it's happening, but it is there. It will make itself known at some point; that I can guarantee.

One of the best things I did for myself was take a chance and move west to Portland back in 2014. As you know, my time there was cut short due to an injury, but that radical move changed my life in ways I never expected. I came back from Portland understanding more of who I was and what I wanted. I came back stronger and more focused. I also finally understood that I could create the life I want no matter the location, and that was an invaluable lesson for me.

It would have been easy for me to stay close to home after losing my job that year, but instead I decided to do something different and take a giant step outside of what I knew to chase a dream.

That kind of drastic move may not be something you can do right now or may not be something you want to do at all, but maybe you have an idea of something similarly radical that you may need to put back on the table and consider. When I left home, the feelings of excitement and hope overshadowed the fear. I knew that the move west would be something I would grow and learn from, and I wanted that. I didn't want to remain the same.

Choosing to step outside the norm forces you to grow as a person. That in itself is so valuable.

Another thing I did that was small but impactful was to give up social media for a month. I don't know where the idea came from or why it was something I felt compelled to do, but I did. The thought kept coming to mind over the course of a few days, and I decided that it was something I needed to do. I thought it would be difficult to let go of, but most days it wasn't. I missed it, but taking thirty days to focus on my projects was a bit of a turning point for me. Nothing super drastic, but at the same time it set me up in ways I didn't expect.

I spent more time with people, which was something I needed. During any season of life, whether you have set out to change your life or not, being around people and connecting with others is important. I lost that for a while. I became a bit of a hermit and breaking that habit and routine was hard to do. I didn't disconnect because I didn't like people—honestly, I love people—but rather because I had set out to protect myself and ended up being alone a lot. During this month of giving up social media, I was intentionally seeking people out and making a point to connect where I could. I knew that one month wouldn't change everything about my social life, I would never expect it to, but it set me on a new path and made me more intentional about connecting with people.

Also during this month, I was able to finish some work on this book and made a point to spend time on some other writing projects I was really excited about. I also sang every day and took pictures of the sky, both things that bring me joy.

Could I have done all the things I did that month without leaving social media behind? Probably. I am sure it was possible to do, but I needed that drastic change in order to get some things sorted out and move forward with certain areas of my life. I was less distracted and more able to do what I needed to do, work on projects that are important to me and make a point of reaching out, which is essential for me.

Sometimes taking something away from your life allows you to make time for the things that are really important to you. Using your time in a new way can open your eyes to what is truly productive and what is wasting your time, as well as show you new ways to make the most of your time.

Giving something up in order to change your life is hard, but it's so amazing in the end. I would recommend that you come up with something that you could give up for a specific amount of time in order to focus your energies on something that is going to move the ball forward. Is there something that is holding you back? Wasting your time? Taking up your energy or keeping you from focusing?

Another great thing to help radically change your life is to seize opportunities that come your way. Instead of being paralyzed with fear or putting them off until the next time they come your way, take advantage. It is so easy to ignore the amazing things that are offered in our lives because of fear. Fear of how people will see us, fear of the work involved, or even fear of the change itself.

It might be easy to judge someone for passing up a great opportunity, but in reality, it is not hard at all to understand why someone might walk away from something good if it is new and outside of their comfort zone. We have all been offered something awesome that is slightly out of our comfort zone, and we sit there questioning whether or not we are capable of this thing. From the outside, someone would say, "Of course, you could do that!" But inside, you wonder if that is true.

Seizing opportunities that come our way is essential for personal growth. Cowering away from every opportunity we get will not do us any favors in the long run. In fact, if we continually resist those amazing things that cross our paths, eventually our confidence could be so eroded that we will never, ever take a step forward and grasp them as they come our way.

One moment that was critical for me as a writer came the fall of 2016. I was freshly laid off from my job and back living with my parents while I was trying to figure out what was next for me. I woke up in the middle of the night and saw that I had a message on Facebook from someone I knew by name only. This person was asking if I was interested in talking to him about possibly writing a freelance article for a local magazine. I remember looking at that message in complete shock and thinking, "This is not in my wheelhouse. I barely blog, I've never published anything, so how could I even consider this?" But I knew I had to do this.

As we talked about the writing gig, which was interviewing a student-athlete, there was this piece of my brain telling me, no matter what, you have to say yes to this. I had never interviewed anyone before, and I am not terribly fluent in sports verbiage, so I was well aware this was outside the norm for me, but I had to do it. I knew that this was an opportunity that I could not turn down. I didn't know if I would ever be asked to do it again, I didn't know how well the interview would go or how I would handle the whole process, but I knew that this moment was important.

So I did it. I figured out a way to plan it out and get through it without allowing myself to go full on into panic mode, and I did it. And it felt good.

The experience stretched me, it challenged me, and though I didn't seek it out, when the chance was there I grabbed it with both hands and put my heart into it even though I was terrified of what I was doing. I wanted to do it, even though I was fearful, even though I was unsure. I wasn't about to let that opportunity pass me by. I have been blessed to be able to do a few more articles for that magazine since then, and I have enjoyed it more each time. In fact, through the process of doing those articles, I have been inspired to start a few more projects as a result. Without taking that chance, I never would have considered some of the things I am doing right now.

Making radical changes—taking a step forward and doing something that scares us a little, helps us move closer to our goals and makes us learn more about ourselves—is an important part of being who we are. It is an important part of growth as an individual.

Trying something new or doing something different isn't always easy and isn't always fun in the beginning. However, the results reveal themselves, and as you start noticing the outcomes of those endeavors, you will become addicted to seizing opportunities instead of shying away from them.

Part of living and having a full life is not continually doing things the same way forever but rather incorporating new things into your life. Trying new things and changing directions can ultimately get you to a place you have never dreamed of before and set brand-new opportunities on your path that will bring you joy that you never expected.

Doing something radical is scary sometimes, and there are moments when it is risky to do so. Whether or not you should step forward in the opportunities that come your way is up to you. It is something you have to weigh and determine on your own. That is not something I can say one way or the other.

What I can tell you is that if you choose not to take a step out, if you choose not to grab onto the worthwhile opportunities that cross your path, chances are you will have some regrets. If you aren't in a season of your life right now where you can say yes, that is one thing. However, if you are just putting things off and saying you'll do them someday or the next time you are offered this chance, you could be hindering your chance to change your life in a big way.

I did not seek out the freelance writing gig. It was a blessing and a gift that I never saw coming. It's likely if I wouldn't have said yes, if I wouldn't have grabbed the opportunity and faced the fear, I may not have been offered something like that again anytime soon and would have missed out.

The process of changing your life requires you to stretch yourself, especially if you want to make big changes. There are going to be moments of discomfort and confusion. There will be times when you question what you are doing and why you are doing it. When you begin to step beyond the things you already know, you are going to see it and feel it without a doubt. Just think of any time you had to learn something new at work or school; your learning curve likely included having to research, ask questions, deal with trial and error and adjust to a new system or idea. This is no different. And if you are bold and brave and choose to do something more radical to make even more drastic changes, you will feel even more amazing.

Radical changes are uncomfortable in one way or another. That cannot be avoided. However, those growing pains are such a gift. They may not feel like it at the time, but I think you would agree with me. Think back to something hard you went through. You struggled, you cried, you fought, and, as a result, you grew, changed, and learned from the experience in some way. That is one of the great benefits of growing pains. I am not saying struggle is a fun process, but the results of the struggle can be quite amazing, granted we choose to see it that way. If we aren't looking for the good, we won't see it.

When you step outside your comfort zone and choose to stretch yourself, there may be some fear involved. It is hard to do something new and not have some of that lurking in the background, or a lot of it in the foreground. It is around, let's just say that. It is also important to reiterate that it is natural, and it is something to be aware of. However, fear should not be an excuse for avoiding making radical changes. It should not be your reason for not making some drastic change to your life to jumpstart your goals or a reason to walk away from a great opportunity. Fear is a healthy response to have, but it should never be your reason for not living a full life or not going after your goals with everything you have.

One of my favorite podcasts is *The Dave Ramsey Show*. I listen to it several times a week, and I love the people that call in or make a trip to their studio in Tennessee to do their debt-free screams. It is so inspiring to hear their stories. The amount of sacrifices they make and the work they put in in order to achieve their goal is so motivating, and not just when it comes to financial aspects but just in life in general. They get radical, to the point that the people in their lives think they are just crazy. They give things up, they learn new skills, and they make things happen. Or, as Dave says, they get hungry for change.[14]

I want you to be hungry in the pursuit of changing your life and achieving the things that matter to you, too. Not just with your finances but in every area of your life. I want there to be a passion behind your journey, a purpose, something that drives you to improve and change and grow. I know I can't just hand something like that over to you; I would if I could. It is something that you have to discover for yourself, something you need to own.

Changing your life is great. Making radical, drastic, upheaval-to-your-life kind of change has the potential of boosting the process. It is just a matter of recognizing when it's appropriate and when it is needed. And that is something only you can determine.

Is it time to do something different? Is it time to give something up or try something new? Maybe it is time to venture into uncharted territory and do something you haven't tried before.

Maybe it's time to shake things up and get a little radical.

Chapter review:

Be willing to step out of your normal routine, habits and comfort zone to challenge yourself a little.

Seize opportunities that come your way, instead of being paralyzed with fear or putting them off until the next time they come your way. Take advantage now!

When you seize opportunities, it can inspire you in ways you never expected.

Fear is a healthy response to have, but it should never be your reason for not living a full life or not going after your goals with everything you have.

Changing your life is great. Making radical, drastic, upheaval-to-your-life kind of change has the potential of boosting the process.

Take action challenge!

Time for another challenge. Are you pumped?

Are you ready to get radical? I know you might not feel ready for it, but shaking up your life can make such a great impact, so I challenge you to take the step forward and do this. What can you change? What can you give up? What are you willing to do in order to advance your life? This is a tough one, I know. However, making sacrifices and stepping outside of your comfort zone will truly change your life in so many ways. You just have to be willing to do it.

Take some time right now to think about what you can do differently, what you can give up, and how you can get a little radical in the process of changing your life!

Take action now!

We can't help everyone, but everyone can help someone.

~ Ronald Reagan

CHAPTER 14

PAY IT FORWARD

One of the best parts about changing your life is that you have a chance to help others. Not just once you have achieved the change you are seeking, but also while you are going through it. You have the opportunity to pay it forward and influence those around you for the better. Your personal growth is a tool you can use to help others do the same. It is such a beautiful thing, going through your own life transformation and then being able to share it with others in a way that helps them become more of what they want to be.

One of the best ways to influence others is by being an example. Live what you say, do what you say. Show them that life can change, situations can change, people can change. Sometimes it is easy to believe that things will never become anything other than what they are right now. Some people are stuck in that mindset and cannot see the possibilities in front of them or their own potential to evolve. Sometimes the best way to learn is by witnessing someone else live out what you hope to accomplish. Sometimes even seeing someone go through a significant change that isn't related to what you want to do impacts a person. I have seen people achieve amazing things that I have never wanted to accomplish myself, but witnessing them go all in and put all of themselves into a passion of theirs has inspired me to do the same with the things that I want to do.

Being willing to share what you have been through to get where you are is something that people will respond to. How many times have you heard someone share a testimony or personal story of overcoming a big obstacle and found yourself inspired? I always walk out of sessions like that just amazed at what this person overcame or what they accomplished and immediately begin to rethink my own doubt about what I am capable of. I begin to think maybe I can conquer the world too. Maybe I can overcome the big obstacle in front of me. Maybe I can achieve more than I realized.

You can be that for someone else. You probably already are and don't even know it, because we often don't know who we make an impact on unless we are told.

I just want to take a quick second to ask you to do the following: if someone has influenced your life in significant ways, if someone has changed the course of your life in some way or given you the courage to step out and do something new, exciting, risky—thank them. Right now, contact them and tell them what they have done for you and how they have changed your life. They deserve to know how much they have impacted you!

In all honesty, you're impacting someone right now. We all affect each other every day, but what I am talking about here is that you are probably changing the course of someone's life in a big way. They are watching the example you are setting and desiring to follow in your footsteps, either to achieve the same things or follow the example you have set while chasing your goals. They see that. They see what you are doing, so don't underestimate the influence you have just by doing what you do every single day.

Share your story, share your journey. Sometimes it can be awkward and uncomfortable to do, especially if things aren't going your way. But truthfully, sometimes that is the best stuff to share. People tend to hide the things that they struggle with when they are trying to change their lives or go after a goal. We would all love to look like we have it all figured out and know everything about everything. We would all like to give off the impression that the journey is a smooth one and we change our lives without a hitch.

We all know that is a lie, but sometimes as outsiders to others' lives, we forget that.

When you are hoping to influence someone or have the opportunity to help someone change their life, one of the first things you should do is build their trust. Be there for them, encourage them. You don't have to be aggressive about it. You don't have to get in their face. Building trust is as easy as following through and keeping your word. If you say you will do something and then fail to do it, the trust is broken. They will not believe you will be there for them when it counts, when they choose to change their life.

Another element of building trust is understanding how people communicate. We all have different personalities and different histories. When life gets complicated or stressful or exciting, we all handle things differently, so understanding how the other person communicates and reacts is going to help you help them.

Another great thing you can do that will make a huge impact on the other person is your ability and willingness to listen to them. Don't listen and think about how you are going to respond at the same time. Focus on what they are saying, hear their words, read their body language and hear their heart. Focus your attention on them and don't let what is going on around you or in your own mind distract you from really understanding where they are coming from and what it is they need to get out. Sometimes a person needs to talk situations out before they can move forward. I do this when I am going through something I am not used to or when I am feeling out of my depth. I reach out to a friend and talk it out, and the ones who understand me the best will offer a few tidbits of advice, but they also know that many times I will get to a resolution on my own just by talking out the situation. You can be that person for someone else. It is a blessing to the other person, believe me. Being a listening ear is huge when it comes to building trust and strengthening relationships. And that can open doors to influencing change when the person is ready.

Influencing and helping others change their lives is something we can all do, and there are so many ways to do it, we just have to choose our actions and approach wisely. It needs to fit the person and the situation, but one thing you can do is show interest in them. Ask them about their goals, their lives, their families, and their hopes for the future. Get the conversation going and find out where their heart is. You never know where it can lead. Help them see their potential. If you notice they have a skill, comment on that. Tell them you noticed how good they are at it and how impressed you were by it. Pay attention to what they do well and support those things. If they have a great habit you've noticed, say something and maybe even ask for their help in that area. Maybe you helping them begins with them helping you learn something new. This is how trust and relationships are built. And this is how we begin to help each other change for the better.

When people are ready to change and want you to be part of their process, let them approach you. Sometimes you can sense that they are ready, but they haven't broached the subject yet. If there is a way you can open the conversation up without scaring them off, do that. But ultimately, the decision to take the step out of theory and thought and into planning and action needs to be theirs and theirs alone. They need to own it fully because it is their life, their responsibility. You can be there for support; in fact, you should be, but this journey needs to belong to them from the get-go.

When they are willing to change, make sure their change is theirs and not yours. You cannot drive their life, and they cannot expect that from you.

Other ways you can influence people is to invite them into your circle. Are you a part of any groups? Do you have a class you take or a meeting you go to on a regular basis? Do you go to seminars that inspire you? Offer to take them with you, to pay for it if you can, and to show them what you are into. Show them what is important to you, what has helped you, and let the presenter speak into their life. Sometimes that can help open the door to what you hope to do in helping someone.

When they begin to change their lives and adjust their goals, be sure to support them. Offer your advice when they are open to it. Keep the line of communication open and practice active listening. Don't be critical when they fail to reach a goal or fall short, rather offer ideas on how they can approach it differently next time. Or just listen to them as they work it out for themselves. And when they achieve a goal, reach a milestone, or make it through a full week of a particular positive activity, celebrate them and celebrate with them. Notice their achievements and tell them how proud you are of them. Encourage the good behavior, the good habits, and the new positive changes they are making when they fall short in some way; resist the urge to criticize them but offer an ear to listen instead.

The opportunity to help others is such a blessing. Being able to show someone else what has helped you get through tough times, overcome a hardship or achieve a long-burning goal is something that we can all do.

It is important to understand that your drive to help others and pay it forward will not always be welcome or understood. You may have the desire to help them, but they may not be in a place where they are ready to be receptive to your help. Don't assume their drive to change is the same as yours. In other words, don't come out full force and scare the pants off someone with your insistence on their need to revamp their life, and don't push them in ways they are just not ready to go. Sometimes you have to wait to be invited in or asked for advice. Letting the other person come to you with questions is often the best way to go.

Something I have seen in people when they choose to change their life is they get on this new bandwagon, a new program, new diet, new lifestyle, new routine, and then begin pushing it on other people. They make the switch from one thing to another and start preaching about what others are doing wrong with their lives or should be doing differently. They believe in the product or process so much, to the point where they are talking down to you. Don't be one of these people. If you are looking to convert people to a way of life or help them become better with this new change you have made, suggest it. Tell people what it is doing for you, share your success in a way that doesn't put them off, and don't start pointing out everything that you think they are doing wrong.

Being critical will not get you the results you are hoping for. Attacking people will not bring them over to the side of change. If you are looking to push people away and help them resist was has helped you, that is your ticket to making that happen.

If they ask for your opinion, give it, but be kind in your responses, so it keeps the conversation going. If they ask for constructive criticism, give it to them. But again, consider your approach and response. You don't want to scare them off and risk losing the opportunity to help them in the future. Or worse, putting them off the idea of asking for help from anyone else down the road.

Remember, your motivation and your hope is to help them live better lives, become better people, and achieve new goals. Don't send them in the other direction because of your reaction.

It is also important to recognize that you cannot change or help everyone. Some people are not interested in change in the least. There are those who are completely satisfied where they are and aren't looking to grow. And that is fine, but you need to be able to see that and not try to push someone into a place they don't have any interest in going. I won't tell you not to waste your time on them, because people are worth investing in no matter what their ambition levels are, however, don't try to push change on them when they have no interest. It will only strain the relationship.

Don't question your ability to influence the people around you. Don't put a limit on what you can do. It is so easy to assume that what we do doesn't matter to anyone. That what we do isn't going to make an impact on people or help anyone. Have you ever felt that way? I know you have, because it is such a common feeling.

There was a time in my life when someone made a point of telling me that I would never be able to help anyone. This person told me that I was too messed up and had too many issues and hang-ups to ever make a difference in anyone's life. And for a long time, I held that to be true. I kept repeating those words in my head over and over, claiming them as personal truths. It took me much too long to let those words go and truly grasp the idea that I was someone who could help others. I am far from perfect, and I have hang-ups and issues just like everyone else, but that does not preclude me from helping someone. And the same goes for you.

It is so easy to start questioning whether we are capable of doing anything that matters to anyone. Would anyone notice if we weren't here? Do the good things we try to do for people make any difference at all?

I am just going to answer that for you right now with a resounding *yes*. Yes, yes, yes.

You impact the people around you, who impact the people around them. What you do, as well as who you are, matters in such a big way. You are valuable, and you have skills, talents, and love to share with the people around you. As I am writing this, I am reminded of a message I received from a friend. And right now, I want to say it to you.

You have so much love and passion, and you have such an amazing and unique perspective on life.
You don't want to keep that all to yourself!
Think about the passion you have put into all the things you want to achieve.
You are amazing.

Don't keep those to yourself. Find ways you can bless those around you and help support them to achieve their goals, realize their dreams, and reach their full potential. Don't buy into the lie that what you are and who you are is insignificant and that you can't help others, because it is a lie.

You have so much to share with the people around you. You have God-given gifts that should be utilized for yourself and to bless others.

Chapter review:

If you take the approach of pushing people to change, more than likely you will get pushback.

Being willing to share what you have been through to get where you are, both the good and the bad, is something that people will respond to, guaranteed.

Build trust with the people you want to help by keeping your word and following through.

Practice active listening when you are helping others. Focus on what they are saying, hear their words, read their body language and hear their heart.

Maybe you helping someone begins with them helping you learn something new.

Take action challenge!

Ready? This is going to be a fun one!

Helping others is such an amazing opportunity that we all need to grab onto and live out! It feels good when you do it, and it is such a blessing to the other person. Think about when you've been helped or guided and how amazing you felt afterward. This is your chance to do this for someone else. Since paying it forward is such a big deal, I am going to ask you to do two challenges.

First of all, if you haven't reached out to someone who has impacted your life in a positive way as I suggested earlier - that person who has changed your life and given you the courage to step out and do something you always wanted to do - I challenge you to do that now. Don't put this one off. Write an email, make a call, send a text, say something on social media or even write them a letter. We often forget to thank those who impact our lives, so don't let this one go another second!

The second thing I want to ask you to do is to approach a friend of yours and ask how you can help them with a goal they might have. Another option is to ask them how you can support them in some way. How awesome would it be if one of your friends did that for you? You can make a difference in someone's life by asking for specific ways you can support them.

Take action now!

The first step towards getting somewhere is to decide that you are not going to stay where you are.

~ J.P. Morgan

CONCLUSION

TAKE OWNERSHIP

Change is not easy. We all know this, and you've read it over and over in this book. We know that the process we need to go through to get to the next level is going to be a challenge. How many times have you tried to change something deeply ingrained in your life? How many times have you tried to change a habit that you just can't get rid of or a relationship that just never seems to get better? Maybe you're in a financial situation that is rough, and you don't see the light at the end of the tunnel. Maybe you're living in a location that doesn't suit you. Maybe your faith or spiritual life is suffering in some way, and you've been trying to change that and haven't quite figured out how to move forward.

Whatever it is you're trying to change, we know that any tools you can grab hold of and apply to your life are going to make that process of changing so much simpler. It may not always be easy, but they could help you move forward and accomplish goals you never thought possible. That is my hope for you as you've read this book. I hope that you have found tools and ideas that have sparked something inside of you to move forward in some way.

My hope and prayer are that you feel more equipped to move forward and change your life, become the person that you want to be, live the life you were meant to live, do the things you want to do, and glorify God in the process. You have gifts to use; you are an asset to this world. And I don't want you to doubt yourself anymore.

You are valuable.

We have covered a lot of things in this book. I have one more thing to share with you, but first, let's review what we have already covered.

You can choose to begin today. You can make decisions to remain in one place and settle in this position that you're in, or you can analyze where you are right now and use that as motivation to get further ahead in life. This is a new beginning for you. Grasp onto this fresh start you have right now, right at this moment, today.

Taking advantage of the time we have builds momentum and gets us moving forward. The more we move forward and utilize that time, the further we get and the faster we get to our goals. Many of the changes in life we desire do not happen overnight. They happen over a period of time. Utilize your time and see your life change.

Things happen that we don't expect and usually, at the time, it is most inconvenient. However, that is not an excuse for us to stop moving forward with our lives. It is not an excuse for us to remain in one place and never make the effort we need to. Life happens, and understanding and grasping that truth will help you get through the bumps in the road.

Our situations often change throughout the course of our lives. We change jobs, our friendships change, we add people to our family and lose someone too, we move to a new city, and we lose or gain money. We need to adjust when life changes occur. We need to be willing to change our plans in order to fit what's happening in our lives. Plans need to be dynamic, and the sooner you learn to adjust to that, the better off you will be in your pursuit of changing your life.

We choose how we treat people. Whether they deserve it or not, we have the choice to be positive, to be encouraging, to be understanding, to be a better individual. We have the choice to see obstacles as opportunities and struggles as learning possibilities. It is on us to recognize that. We have the choice of what kind of attitude we are going to have, so choose wisely.

Perfection does not exist. None of us are capable of doing everything perfectly, so it is better for us to focus less on perfection and more on progress. We need to concentrate on the progress we are making, the steps we are taking forward. Pursue progress over perfection.

Surrounding yourself with the right people is vital when it comes to changing your life. You need to have support and encouragement as you take on the challenges in front of you. You also need to remember that not everyone is going to understand your journey. Do not let other people's fears become yours. Do not let your gifts go unused because somebody else doesn't understand your need to use them. Do not let the goals that are stamped on your soul be snuffed out by someone who can't see life from the same point of view as you. Surround yourself with like-minded people, people who pursue the things you pursue and who can support you. Find your people.

Following through on the things you set out to do and the plan you have set up for yourself is one of the best things you can do for yourself when you are on a path to changing your life. Seizing opportunities and moments you have in your day to accomplish small goals in order to accomplish a big goal is monumental in the process. Understand what works for you and what doesn't as well. Your ability to follow through, regardless of your feelings, will get you further much faster. Choose to follow through.

It is important for you to be proud of yourself for the small steps you take forward, those times when you get up earlier in the morning to focus extra time on that project, when you choose to work out, write those extra words, work the extra job, study a language or practice your musical instrument. Whatever it is that you are trying to change and develop in your own life, you need to take moments to be proud of yourself, because that is something worth celebrating. Celebrating your successes and efforts, big and small, will propel you and bring the momentum to a whole new level as you move forward. Don't disregard this step.

Just like choosing our attitude, we have the option to choose joy. We can choice to see the good in the little things that happen throughout our day. We have the choice to search out those things that make us laugh and smile. Even on a Monday morning. Choose to be joyful.

We have to remember that plans need to be dynamic because life is ever changing and our situations can change often. We need to be ready for that. But in the times in between when we have the opportunity to have structure, it is vital to take advantage of that. Having a routine is going to help you focus energy on the things that need to be done. And in turn, this will allow you to get further ahead and create the life that you really want. Choose to utilize the power of routine.

Be willing to ask for help and reach out to people. None of us know everything. Not a single person on the planet can handle every situation without some assistance. We were not meant to go through life alone, and we are not meant to carry our burdens alone. Don't be stubborn and put off reaching out. Don't be too proud to ask for help.

Sometimes you need to step outside your comfort zone in order to make things happen. As scary as that can be, it is a way to shake up results and get clarity. It is a way to get hyper-focused on important things or give up things that are extremely distracting. Getting radical and taking advantage of opportunities that come your way can be the ultimate boost for making big changes you are trying to make. Is it time for you to take this step?

You are going to gain so much knowledge and experience as you go through the process of changing your life, and that is something that you should use to help others. You should pass on what you learn to help the people in your life. You should also share your journey getting to your goal as well. There's something so inspiring about watching someone go through a change that is hard and seeing what happens after the fact is inspiring as well. Pay it forward and help others.

And now, we get to the last part of this journey.

It is time to take ownership.

It is time to own your journey. It is time to own your choices. It is time to own your attitude, outlook, and actions. No one can make the choices for you. No one can carry this journey for you. People can support, encourage and cheer you on, but ultimately this process belongs to you and only you.

You need to take possession and protect your goals. You need to begin, utilize your time, and understand that life happens when we least expect it to. You need to understand that plans need to be dynamic, that you choose your attitude and that progress is better than perfection. You need to seek support, follow through on your plans and take the time to celebrate your efforts. You need to choose joy, utilize routines, and ask for help. You need to get radical. You need to pay it forward.

You.

You need to take ownership of your journey. You are driving the ship. You are in charge. The responsibility for creating a new life, becoming a better person, learning a new skill and achieving personal growth lies squarely on your shoulders.

Yours.

Change is hard. Change is a difficult road that we all should go down; none of us should stay where we are, as comfortable as it might be. We need to travel down this road in order to become better people. It is our duty to continually work on using the gifts we have been given and share them with others. We were never meant to stay the same forever.

CHOOSE CHANGE

I don't know where you're at right now. I don't know what you have to change. I don't know what struggles you have or what challenges you face every day. I don't know who you are, what your passions are, or what your personality type is, but there are two things I'm certain of.

First of all, I care for you deeply. I don't know what your face looks like or what your voice sounds like, but your life matters to me. You matter to me. I want the best for you, and I want you to accomplish all the great things that you have in your heart. I want you to use your gifts to help yourself and the other people in your life. You are a unique person, you are a special person, and you are capable of so much. My hope is that you believe and see that for yourself as well.

Second, I believe you are capable of great change. So many of the goals you have for your life, so many of the things that you dream about at night or daydream about during the day are possible. Not everyone is going to see it the way you do, but I do. You may have doubts right now about what you are capable of, but I know with all of my heart that change is possible for you. And that it is worth putting the effort in to achieve it.

What do you want your life to look like? What do you want your future to look like? What is it that keeps you up at night, what is the dream that won't let you go? What are you unhappy with? What do you want to improve on?

You have a chance to start right now, today. Seize this opportunity; don't let it pass.

Lean into it, and keep pushing.

Take action challenge!

You better be ready for the biggest challenge yet!

Yes, that is what I said. It is time to start changing your life! If you haven't started taking action yet, it is now time to truly begin and to embrace the process of changing your life. It is time to put into action the things you have learned.

It is so easy to remain in the same place. It is so easy to keep putting things off and just hope for things to be different. Don't do that. Don't waste time and energy wishing things into existence; take action and make things happen. It is time to take the bull by the horns and make things happen.

It is time to change your life.

Take action now!

MESSAGE FROM THE AUTHOR

As I was working on this book, one of my favorite songs came on, and I sat there mesmerized by the music and the words. Toward the end of the song, I realized how fitting it was for this book, so I thought I would share a portion of the song with you here.

This is a song that I love dearly, so much so that I got the title tattooed on my foot. The song is "I'm the Proof" by Ed Kowalczyk. So many of the songs he has written, both as a solo artist and as a member of Live, have touched my heart in various ways. This one in particular is at the top of my list of favorite songs. Here is a portion of the song:

(bridge)
Lay it down
All your pain
All your fear
All your sorrow

Lay it down
All your tears
All your worry for tomorrow

Lay it down
Come on out
Let the sun shine on your face

CHOOSE CHANGE

Lay it down
Lay it down
I know you're ready

***

(chorus)
If you were, well I was too
Where you've gone, I've been there
I've chased that fire but I found the truth

But sometimes people change,
And I'm the proof

I spent a lot of time thinking that my life could never be what I wanted it to be. That I couldn't be what God called me to be. I was heartbroken over that belief. I wanted something different, something better, something more fulfilling, but I could never find my way there. I fought to keep myself from spiraling downward, but it never seemed to hold for very long.

Eventually, I found the truth that I could change.

The choices I was making were getting me to places I didn't want to be, but I could change the direction of my life with God's help. I could choose a different path, and that realization opened up my world. I didn't have to be depressed all the time. I didn't have to be filled with anxiety. I didn't have to believe all the lies I was being fed and feeding myself. I didn't have to be stuck.

However, it was up to me to make the changes and step forward.

Has the journey been perfect? Far from it. I reached this point of realization fifteen years ago, but it has been a battle to continue to hold onto this truth, though it has become easier with time.

And the truth is, I don't even know if people can see the change from the outside. But change doesn't have to be flashy. It can be something quiet within your heart, a truth you hold onto and live out without making a big announcement. Whether it's deep inside you or something you live out loud, your journey to change is a powerful one that can impact others.

Is it time to lay down your fear, your regret of the past, your sorrow, and your worry? Is it time to live the life you were called to live and use the gifts you were given to bless others? That is a question only you can answer, and I pray you can answer it with a resounding "YES!"

You are capable of change. There is no doubt in my mind. You are capable of making things happen. You are capable of moving the mountains in your life.

Let's go on this journey together.

I know you're ready.

CHAPTER CHALLENGES

Are you ready to take the challenges? Are you ready to take some steps forward to changing your life for the better? Here is the full list of chapter challenges for you to work through! Be bold and start changing your life today!

Intro
What are your dreams? Your ambitions? Your goals? What do you want to change about your life? How would you like to improve your situation or help to improve the lives of others? Write it all down, and don't leave anything out!

1
What small steps can you take today to start improving your life? A few ideas would be adding a ten-minute walk to your morning, writing 500 words in the book you've always wanted to publish, reading a few pages of an inspiring book, eating some extra fruits or vegetables, or encouraging a friend. Sometimes it feels like changing our lives needs to be big and complicated, but the truth is it doesn't need to be. Take out a piece of paper and a pen right now and start brainstorming some ideas! What is something small you can do every day that will help you create the life you want?

2
As we have discussed, utilizing your time is a major step in changing your life. So let me ask you, are you utilizing yours? Take a minute right now to think about your day and how you structure it. Are you making the most of your

time in order to get closer to your goals? Could you use your lunch hour differently? Could you arrive earlier, or stay a little later? Could you give up one of your favorite TV shows or cut back on a certain hobby in order to take a step forward to creating a better life for yourself?

What could you do to utilize your time better starting today?

3

Have you had any new changes in your life? Has life blindsided you recently? Maybe it is time to take stock of where you are and what your priorities need to be. It is so easy to get distracted from your goals when something changes unexpectedly. Do you need to take a break from your goals to reassess? Or have you been on the sidelines for a while and need to get back to work on your goals?

Take a moment to think about your current situation and decide what your next move needs to be.

4

So, we have just discussed how plans need to be dynamic because life is ever changing. Have you hit a point where your plans to move forward don't seem to make sense anymore? What has recently changed that is causing you to question your current path? And one more question. Are you fighting to hold onto a plan that needs to be changed or abandoned for a new one? I know how hard it is to adjust your goals and plans when unexpected things happen, but I challenge you to take time right now to think about these questions and answer them for yourself.

Don't get stuck in a loop and hold onto things that aren't working.

5

Our attitudes are so powerful. How we approach people and talk to ourselves can change the direction and focus of our day. It is truly amazing. Are you struggling with your attitude? Are you feeling weighed down and burdened by it? Is there a relationship you have that is making it hard for you to be positive at home or work? I want to challenge you, right now, to think about that situation. What can you do to improve it? What choices can you make to improve the situation and begin to take control of your attitude?

6

The process of change is a tough one and chasing the idea of perfection makes it that much harder! It is time to let that go, don't you think? I have a challenge for you. What if you were to sit down tonight and make a list of all the things you did today in order to move toward a better life? What would that list include? Take out a piece of paper and write down what you have accomplished in the past twenty-four hours that has improved your situation. If you want to take it a step further, commit to doing this for the next seven days.

Not only will it feel good to see what you have accomplished, but it will also give you insight into which tasks are more important and which are getting you closer to the life you want to create for yourself.

7

It is important for everyone to have people they can count on in all seasons of life, whether or not they are on a journey to change their life. And that includes YOU! Do you have a group of people you can count on? Do you have the support you need to move forward with your goals? This is something I want to encourage you to pursue with some intention. So often, our goals fall by the wayside because we do not surround ourselves with like-minded people and end up losing our momentum. It is time for you to expand your circle!

Take a minute to think about what your goals are and then think of ways to actively seek out people who are after the same or similar goals. Is there a group you can join? Or create? Are there people at your church or place of employment you can connect with? There are people out there! Seek out support!

8

Change takes effort. Simple as that. And sometimes, not so simple. It is much easier to say than do, isn't it? Like most things in life, it takes time and continual follow-through. So, let's practice it! Like any change we want to make, there is an end goal in mind. To become the best or better at something or to create a new habit. What I am going to challenge you to do right now is to choose that thing you want to become more consistent at following through on. Could be working on a skill, reading a few pages of a book, writing a few words, exercising, encouraging friends, cooking healthy meals, or a number of another things.

I want you to commit right now to taking the first step forward and decide you are going to do this activity for seven days. It may not become a habit in that time frame, but if you look back and realize what you were able to accomplish and feel the great feelings that come along with that, I know you'll feel amazing and want to continue.

9

This is one of my favorite challenges, and one of my favorite things to do every day! It is so easy for us to get to the end of the day and think that we didn't accomplish anything or that we didn't get any closer to our goals that day. This activity can help you refocus and see if you are choosing actions that will get you closer to your goals.

What I want you to do is take out a sheet of paper and a pen and place it on your nightstand. For the next seven days, just after you crawl into bed, write down three things you did that day to improve your life. Did you eat right? Save money? Exercise? Invest in a relationship or friendship? Make a sale? Write a few words? There could be so many different things you could list here.

Commit yourself to doing this for a full seven days. I think you'll see how powerful it can be and that there is much to celebrate!

10

We all have someone in our lives that brings us down in some way, whether they mean to or not. Those kinds of relationships are challenging and frustrating and can really become a burden to bear. Whether you are in that place right now or not, I want you to start thinking about how you can deal with those people in your life. It is important to have a game plan on how you are going to keep your joy when you are around people who seem determined to bring you down. That is what I want to challenge you to do right now. This isn't always an easy task, but it is an important one.

The best way to figure out how to deal with this situation is to ask yourself some questions. Why is this person acting this way? Why are they treating me like this? Am I doing something to make the situation worse? Am I encouraging it somehow? Is this something I can talk to them about?
From there, you can formulate a plan on how you can approach this person and situation in the best way. Don't

assume every tack you take will work with every person. It is important for you to do this on a person-to-person basis. Start writing down some ideas you have! And take action!

11

What I want you to do is choose something you want to improve on or a skill you want to acquire. What is something you want to add to your life? What skill are you lacking? What activity do you want or need to spend more time on, either for fun or productivity? I am going to leave this open for you to decide because ultimately, this needs to fit into the life you want to create for yourself.

Now, set aside a half hour every day for this one particular thing you have chosen to do. It can be in the morning, afternoon or evening. The timing doesn't matter as much as the follow-through. You know when you are at your best to complete it, and you also know when you have time for it. Spend a half hour each day for seven days and see what happens. The more you do it, the more results you will see.

12

When we are looking to grow as people or in our skills, asking for help is always part of that picture. We can learn things on our own by reading or observing, but truthfully, connecting to another person just ups the ante and impacts our lives even more. This challenge right here is something that took me over a year to do myself. I thought about it and thought about it and finally stepped out of my comfort zone, and honestly, I wish I wouldn't have waited so long! It is time to ask for help.

Do you want a mentor? Do you want someone to help you learn a skill, talk you through tough situations or help you become a better leader? Who could be that person for you?

Take some time to think about what it is you need help with and who could help you with it, then approach them. Don't put it off for as long as I did. You know what you need, and I'm betting they will be willing to help you. Step out and ask for help!

13

Are you ready to get radical? I know you might not feel ready for it, but shaking up your life can make such a great impact, so I challenge you to take the step forward and do this. What can you change? What can you give up? What are you willing to do in order to advance your life? This is a tough one, I know. However, making sacrifices and stepping outside of your comfort zone will truly change your life in so many ways. You just have to be willing to do it.

Take some time right now to think about what you can do differently, what you can give up, and how you can get a little radical in the process of changing your life!

14

Helping others is such an amazing opportunity that we all need to grab onto and live out! It feels good when you do it, and it is such a blessing to the other person. Think about when you've been helped or guided and how amazing you felt afterward. This is your chance to do this for someone else. Since paying it forward is such a big deal, I am going to ask you to do two challenges.

First of all, if you haven't reached out to someone who has impacted your life in a positive way as I suggested earlier - that person who has changed your life and given you the courage to step out and do something you always wanted to do - I challenge you to do that now. Don't put this one off. Write an email, make a call, send a text, say something on social media or even write them a letter. We often forget to thank those who impact our lives, so don't let this one go another second!

The second thing I want to ask you to do is to approach a friend of yours and ask how you can help them with a goal they might have. Another option is to ask them how you can support them in some way. How awesome would it be if one of your friends did that for you? You can make a difference in someone's life by asking for specific ways you can support them.

Conclusion

Yes, that is what I said. It is time to start changing your life! If you haven't started taking action yet, it is now time to truly begin and to embrace the process of changing your life. It is time to put into action the things you have learned.

It is so easy to remain in the same place. It is so easy to keep putting things off and just hope for things to be different. Don't do that. Don't waste time and energy wishing things into existence; take action and make things happen. It is time to take the bull by the horns and make things happen.

It is time to change your life.

QUOTE INSPIRATION

There are many things that I love, and one of those things happens to be inspirational and motivational quotes. I truly believe that words have power and I wanted to share a few of my favorite quotes with you.

Write them down and place them on your bathroom mirror, on your refrigerator, or on your computer screen at the office to inspire you.

It is important to make a point to remind yourself of things that are true, so you are more equipped to fight the false thoughts you may have.

Choose change!

> You change your life by changing your heart.
> ~ Max Lucado

> Strength and growth come only through continuous effort and struggle.
> ~ Napoleon Hill

> Progress is impossible without change, and those who cannot change their minds cannot change anything.
> ~ George Bernard Shaw

> No matter what people tell you, words and ideas can change the world.
> ~ Robin Williams

CHOOSE CHANGE

You cannot change your destination overnight, but you can change your direction overnight.
~ Jim Rohn

Your entire life changes the day you decide you will no longer accept mediocrity for yourself.
~ Hal Elrod

Only I can change my life. No one can do it for me.
~ Carol Burnett

Leaders are made, they are not born. They are made by hard effort which is the price which all of us must pay to achieve any goal that is worthwhile.
~ Vince Lombardi

Successful people do whatever it takes to get the job done, whether or not they feel like it.
~ Jeff Olson

You are far too smart to be the only thing standing in your way.
~ Jennifer J. Freeman

ACKNOWLEDGEMENTS

I am so thankful for the encouragement and help I have received during this process. I couldn't have asked for better people in my life. To each of you, I hope to support you in a similar way someday!

Lana, I am so thankful for your friendship! You are a kindred spirit and like a sister to me. I can't imagine life without you! Thank you for supporting and pushing me to pursue the calls on my heart! And for being an example for me to follow!

Lise, you said one day I would write a book, and here it is! Thank you for pushing me and believing in me. Your friendship is so precious to me, and I hope you know how much I love you!

Carrie, thank you for working with me on this project! I appreciate your honesty and help a great deal! I am grateful for all the work you did! Love ya, girl!

ABOUT THE AUTHOR

Angela Garvin is a blogger and writer who is passionate about helping people better understand themselves and transform their lives. She has spent over a decade learning and researching of personal development and self-improvement tips and tricks to better her own life, and now the lives of others! Angela lives in Minnesota with her pet turtle, Oz, and enjoys spending time with her family, including her four nieces.

Be sure to connect with her on
www.amgarvin.com, Facebook, and Instagram!

And then head over to Facebook to join the
Choose Change Mastermind Community!

RESOURCES

[1] https://www.merriam-webster.com/dictionary/change. Accessed 7 January 2018.

[2] https://en.oxforddictionaries.com/definition/progression. Accessed 7 January 2018.

[3] "Home Again, Rose, Part 1." 1992. *Golden Girls,* season 7, episode 23, Buena Vista Home Entertainment, Inc., 2007, disc 3.

[4] Olson, Jeff. *The Slight Edge*. SUCCESS, 2005-2013, p. 65.

[5] https://www.merriam-webster.com/dictionary/momentum. Accessed 7 January 2018.

[6] Baer, Drake. "Malcolm Gladwell Explains What Everyone Gets Wrong About His Famous '10,000 Hour Rule.'" Business Insider, http://www.businessinsider.com/malcolm-gladwell-explains-the-10000-hour-rule-2014-6. Accessed 7 January 2018.

[7] https://www.merriam-webster.com/dictionary/failure. Accessed 7 January 2018.

[8] Corder, Honorée. *Vision to Reality*. Honorée Enterprises Publishing, LLC., 2014, p. 17.

[9] http://www.dictionary.com/browse/perfect. Accessed 7 January 2018.

[10] Elrod, Hal, host. "The ONE Thing You Can Do to Master All Areas of Life with Jay Papasan." *Achieve Your Goals with Hal Elrod*, episode 164. http://halelrod.com/jay-papasan-on-the-one-thing-you-can-do-to-master-all-areas-of-life/.

[11] LaMeaux, E.C. "7 Health Benefits of Laughter." Gaiam, https://www.gaiam.com/blogs/discover/7-health-benefits-of-laughter. Accessed 7 January 2018.

[12] Elrod, Hal. *The Miracle Morning*. Hal Elrod International, 2014. Print.

[13] Goins, Jeff. *You are a writer*. Tribe Press, 2012, pp. 27-28.

[14] The Dave Ramsey Show. "Be HUUUNGRY." Online video clip. YouTube. YouTube, 5 July 2016. Web. 7 January 2018.

SO GRATEFUL!

Thank you for purchasing my book!

I appreciate all of your feedback and support, and I love hearing what you have to say.

If you have enjoyed this book, I would appreciate it if you would write a review on Amazon!

Thank you so much!

~ Angela

Made in the USA
Columbia, SC
09 July 2018